D0948734

THE DOG IN ACTION

The
Dog in Action

A study of Anatomy and Locomotion
as applying to all breeds

By
McDOWELL LYON

ILLUSTRATIONS BY AUTHOR

SIXTEENTH PRINTING

1982
HOWELL BOOK HOUSE INC.
230 Park Avenue
New York, N.Y. 10169

ISBN 0–87605–468–8

Contents

vii

Illustrations

Introduction

FANCIERS will concede the study of the dog to be a very worthwhile pursuit, even though they regard him as a Pointer, a Pom, or whatever kind of dog they happen to possess. So enthusiastic is the average fancier today over the beauty and the wonder of his own dog that he sees him for the most part as the exponent of a breed unique among all other breeds; to him, other breeds may not even exist.

In one way, intense enthusiasm is a good thing for, without it, breeds of dogs might not have attained their really startling development through artificial selection. In certain other respects, unrestrained breed loyalty can lead to an impasse where we forget that our dog is as any other dog, a mite different perhaps in a superficial way but fundamentally the same as all the rest. And so by too close application to the breed, we neglect full appreciation of the dog as an animal, which is more important because it is basic.

There are two kinds of canine study: the surface, which is the appearance or characterization of a breed, and the working parts beneath the surface together with the mechanical laws governing them. Appearance is no more than eye appeal. Go under the skin if you would answer the riddle of build and operation! Once we understand the reason for feature and action, and the effect which variations cause, the more truly can we evaluate what meets the eye, and then winnow the important from the less important trends of fancy.

In this volume the author takes no account of the dog as a winner in the show room; he is but moderately interested in his appearance as a Pointer or as a Pomeranian. Instead, he is deeply concerned as regards physical make-up for the proper functioning of the Pointer as a Pointer, and of the Pom as a Pom.

The value of a book lies in the ability of the reader to use the information given. In this case, such use will depend upon the true interpretation of terms handed down through generations to dog people—terms like "sloping shoulders," "hocks let down," "back line," "bone," and so on. These are too readily regarded as purely *pictorial,* as referring to the dog's visible outline. They should be recognized, however, as *factorial* because they constitute some of those under-the-skin mechanics directly influencing *both form and function.* The object of our study, then, is not alone to recognize these qualities on a basis of appearance, but to learn the effect which the degree of their existence produces, and then to apply the knowledge to the breed under scrutiny.

To get the best out of this book, the reader will have to discard the idea that his breed is different, and that in consequence he need not acquire a knowledge of principles that may be illustrated by some other breed. The straight shoulder blade, for example, functions mechanically the same on one animal as on another, so when we understand the manner of shoulder blade function we can proceed from that point and use upon any breed at all the knowledge gained.

For the purpose of assisting the reader in this study of anatomy and locomotion, there is appended a glossary where each term used is simply defined. We sincerely trust that the reader will make such constant reference to these listed explanations as may be required for perfect understanding.

The author is to be congratulated on giving to the fancy a kind of book it has not enjoyed heretofore—a study of the dog from the inside out, which should prove of inestimable service to artist, breeder and judge.

JOSEPHINE Z. RINE

My appreciation is here extended to the *American Kennel Gazette* for permission to reprint the portions of this book originally published in that magazine.

THE AUTHOR.

1

Dog Engineers

As a magnificent Pointer moved over the level turf at a leading dog show, it was easy to see that my venerable companion did not regard him highly. There was that expression on his face that seemed to mirror a mouse peeping out of the cupboard.

"Well, what's wrong with him?" I challenged.

"Hum-m," the old man grunted, "he's running uphill."

That seemed so enigmatic that I asked for an explanation.

"His shoulders are taking as much punishment on level ground as well placed ones should in going uphill. He would not have much endurance afield."

I watched the dog move to and fro, then shook my head. "I still don't get it. What's your explanation and authority?"

"My authority!" he snorted, more than a little irritated. "Huh, nature and common sense—they are my authority." Then the expression of his gray eyes softened with tolerance. "Son, unless you know what is taking place beneath the skin and coat of a dog when he moves and the forces he is overcoming, you would not understand the explanation. And if you do know that, you will not need an explanation. Do you honestly know what part a shoulder plays in a dog's gait?"

"But the standards—"

"Yes, the standards," he went on without waiting for my defense, "were originally written by men who had a sound knowledge of dogs and also horses under working conditions. Unfortunately few of us today have the knowledge that comes from actual experience. The breeder knows that the standard asks for a certain feature—he is not always positive just what that is because the terms do not give him a true picture. Even fewer know why the feature is desirable. Despite that, breeders seem to be pretty fair mechanics though poor engineers."

"Dogs are not put together like a machine! So I don't see what a mechanic has to do with it."

"Simply this: a mechanic might do a good job erecting a bridge from a blueprint and specifications without giving a hoot as to why it was so designed. On the other hand, the engineer knows the reason for each piece of steel being so placed, and he appreciates the effect that any slight change might have on the strength of the whole structure."

That conversation took place more than 25 years before this writing was completed but it dated the beginning of this research. Even in the beginning, it seemed plausible that there were sound, mechanical reasons for each physical factor, though it be a virtue in one and a fault in another. Understanding its value to one breed gave a clearer appreciation of its fault in the other.

As we neared the answer to these questions we realized that, far from making any new discoveries, any good judge at field trials or bench shows recognized these factors. Some may have analyzed them completely; others perhaps arrived at them solely through years of contact and experience, the process of elimination by comparison.

The judge or breeder who knows the desired features solely by the rule of thumb will do a good job, but the one who understands the underlying principles should be more reliable in close decisions.

It is one thing to recognize a high-set tail when seen in the ring and another to know its real advantage to the function of the dog's parts. The judge or breeder who is conscious of the mechanical advantage of the fill-in before the eyes of a terrier will not so easily compromise with a half-fill. It is such knowledge that all breeders should seek.

STANDARDS ARE SPECIFICATIONS

We take no issue with standards. For the purpose they serve, the majority are written as they should be though some could be more explicit. One cannot expect a canine education by reading a tabulation of the characterizing features of a breed. Standards are patterns in words, often vague and always elastic. Many depend on terms that came from the paddock while the average breeder's knowledge of horses is limited to the scratch sheet or to watching the bang-tails tossed like dice on the tracks. At best, a standard can only be considered a written specification.

The actual blueprint that comes before the breeder's eyes is the winning dog he sees in the show ring. This cre-

You have to go behind a breed's description to learn the answer to the blueprint described in the standards or paraded in the show ring.

ates a mental picture for him—the projection in flesh of the specifications. However, this animal might have a cardinal structural fault and win in spite of it because the others are just as bad or because the fancy at that time is emphasizing special characteristics. In such a case the breeder is apt to form a mental blueprint that is not sound, and as time passes the fault becomes an earmark of the breed or of his own animals.

Several years ago, a novice received as a gift a show winning dog that he affectionately called "My old Boy," and he soon became an enthusiastic fancier of the breed, eventually acquiring a judge's license. As we found him stewarding for another judge, we chatted with him across the ropes.

"I like the dog he has in number two spot," he said with enthusiasm. "Watch him move. He has a front just like My Old Boy—it's been a long time since I've seen one that good."

The crux of this statement was that his Old Boy had blades far too small and lying as much on his neck as his ribs; so did his choice in the ring. Down through the years, he has probably carried the memory of that first dog as an indelible impression of what a good dog should be like, particularly the ideal front. Perhaps someone in whom he then had confidence assured him the dog was excellent in that feature and he never tried to analyze it.

With such specifications as the standards give and the blueprints present in the ring, even a good mechanic might have difficulty in erecting a bridge. Therefore a profound knowledge of dogs is required to interpret any standard. It is that which lies behind a breed's description which is of consequence. Every student of a breed should become familiar with both background and mechanical factors involved in each feature.

"Why is such a study worthwhile," it has been asked,

"except for academic interest? And, unless we are to be a pedagog, why that interest?"

The study may not be worthwhile for the man satisfied to purchase show winners on their own and their agents' judgment, or dogs bred from those winners. Neither would it be for the buyer of a pet-shop dog, nor the average house-pet owner. This is based on the truism that one need not be a textile expert to purchase the latest style suit displayed in popular stores. However, the man who is producing or buying dogs will do much better with a sound knowledge of what he is trying to secure; for him it is expedient to become academic.

You cannot reach this goal as simply as one breeder desired. "I don't have the time for all that. It doesn't make much difference to me why a front is good just so it is good. Tell me how to breed good ones on my dogs— that'll be enough."

There is no easy road to anything worthwhile. We get out of a venture approximately what we put into it. How could this breeder have hoped to get good fronts without knowing the factors that made a good front? Such an understanding might prevent many of us from becoming cross-eyed when looking at our own dogs.

PERFORMANCE MAKES THE PLANS

A standard describes a dog in parts and its physical attributes. It does not deal with mentality or other characteristics which are related to that. In the show ring, we judge these physical features singly and in comparison with one another. In the field, we judge them on performance or ability to function.

Where a standard makes a statement such as, "hocks near the ground, the dog standing well up on them," we can be certain that there was a mechanical reason for this. Certainly we will appreciate, "Shoulders should be long and sloping, well laid back," much better if we know that a blade set at 45 degrees is 25 per cent more efficient than one standing at 60 degrees.

"That takes us to working problems," a breeder protests, "and our dogs don't work any more."

It is true that few spaniel owners ever shoot over their dogs, that thousands of terriers live and die without a glimpse of a groundhog, that Dalmatians are not running between buggy wheels any more, and that the Collie's only contact with sheep may be a carved leg of mutton from the ice box. It is also true that the ability of a Dal to do six miles an hour for the better part of the day, if you had the buggy wheels, will not detract from his beauty. The field dog which can streak across the meadow in a level gallop loses none of his attraction because of that conformation.

The great Man O'War, Eighty-thirty, Twenty Grand and a host of other horses have been just as pleasing to the eye, built as race horses should be, as if they had followed some quirk of fashion and spent their lives nudging apples out of your hand and posing for admiration. There is nothing tawdry about real ability to perform and we can only breed performance in our dogs by a sound knowledge as to what it takes to make them tick.

The toy dogs too, though bred for fancy alone, must perform. And the house dog must move, at least from lap to feed pan and back to lap by way of an outspread newspaper. The running gear of the average toy has been deficient for many years and it will take concentrated effort along with an understanding of the purpose for each part to put him where he should be and where many breeders want him.

"Times have changed," another contends. "Our dogs are no longer used for those old-fashioned customs. We are breeding dogs for modern conditions and must bring the standards up-to-date to meet the modern dog we are creating."

There is no reason for not changing standards when conditions call for a deviation from the old. New standards and changes will always be in the offing. But whatever changes do take place should not impose a locomotive hardship on the dog.

To illustrate this, we might glance at the Dachshund Standard which says of the front: *Joint between forearm and foot (wrists): these are closer together than the shoulder joints, so that the front does not appear absolutely straight.* The originators of this breed did not write that in because they liked a bent leg but because it served a mechanical purpose, so if modern breeders should choose to make the Dachs' front appear straight they will have to do something about the transverse placement of the shoulder blade or throw the assembly out of dynamic balance.

Another illustration is found in the English Setter, originally a field-going-bird-finding dog whose purpose in life was not questioned. They reach their peak of performance at the annual National Pointer and Setter Stake, run

As well run one of Colonel Ames' milk cows with the Pointers and Setters at Grand Junction as the average bench show specimen.

for years over the estate of Colonel Ames at Grand Junction, Tennessee. The bench show winners would look as out of place with these dogs as would one of Colonel Ames' milk cows because they are incapable of a sustained level gallop.

If the breeders of these dogs reached this end intentionally, knowing all along what the upright shoulder blades would do to the dog's gait afield, we would not discredit their purpose. Where deviations occur, the advocates should be well aware of the reflective effect on other parts of the dog, and prevent or compensate for any ineptitudes whether they disqualify or not.

THE TYPE OF THE DOG

Cliques do form among fanciers, with or without intent, that change the popular types of the dogs which they breed. The dog that wins in the show ring is quite naturally the "type of the day." Other breeders and owners become reconciled to this type by association. Had we been raised among tin cans we would not consider them trash. Spring styles may look freakish when first flashed upon us but anything else is old-fashioned by the advent of autumn.

This popular demand is apt to be a figment, a product of propaganda. The general public accepts this because it is not grounded, and never will be, in the factors that make a dog tick. With blind faith in some "successful" breeder, it will accept a sickle-hocked dog as readily as one standing well up on hocks because it does not know the meaning or reasons for either.

It is true that dogs cannot be bred to a positive blueprint or judged with "mikes" and a tape. However, we can know what we are doing and why we are doing it. If we do, we will forget that there are bench, field and working types with variations of each.

Some time ago, a friend insisted that I must look at a then winning dog.

"You must watch his rear action going away," he beamed, "it's marvelous! His back legs move absolutely parallel to each other."

He was right; the legs did move perpendicular to the ground with no effort to get his pads under his body's center of gravity. Perhaps, had the dog put his pads under

Perhaps we should breed our dogs for modern conditions—even to sprawling with a highball on a lounge seat atop a penthouse roof.

that center for better body support, my friend would have said that he moved too close. If we do not know the mechanical factors involved, our idea is not so apt to be sound.

The man who knows the mechanical support that the "fill-in" before the eyes of a terrier gives the "cutting molars" will never compromise on a snipy face. The one who appreciates the fact that a shoulder blade laid back 45 degrees is 25 per cent more efficient than a 60-degree layback will not be satisfied with the 70-degree blades seen on so many dogs.

Perhaps we should breed our dogs for modern conditions, even to sprawling with a highball on a chaise-longue atop a penthouse roof. Some breeds do owe their general characteristics to fancy alone, though the requisites of natural work are still marks of beauty in many. The majority of breeds won their original popularity by their ability to perform; they evolved without any particular planning on the part of man as to detailed features. Certain individuals had the ability to perform some task useful to man and were mated to others possessing the same ability. It was only after action became fixed that minute features received attention.

ORIGIN AND PURPOSE ARE BASIC

Whatever feature seemed to do the best job was emphasized by the breeder and soon became a fixed part of the dog. The conditions under which the dog worked were responsible for both these and the variations found in the same breed. For instance, in some sections rough-coated retrievers became caked with ice on frosty mornings and the hunters preferred the smooth coats. The duck's keen eye in detecting the reflected light from the slick coats prompted others to choose the rough, non-reflecting coat that matched the waterside growth in color and this even changed with geography.

More care was given to the selection of physical conformation than to coat in the majority of breeds. These original breeders may not have known the laws of leverage or that a center of gravity existed, but they did know what it took to make a performer and they had the chance to prove their point in the field. These men also showed that they had a sound knowledge of all dogs and not of just one breed, and that they were generally well acquainted with horses. The very wording which they employed in their standards gives evidence to these facts.

Often we must go back to the origin of breeds to find the reasons for certain features. Certainly the pants of the Afghan were not put on because some Rajah blushed at a Greyhound's nakedness. The high speed, straight running Pointers and Setters seen at American field trials do not indicate that Americans are more vigorous hunters than their Continental cousins who prefer the closer working, zigzag casting dogs.

Beneath all these variations, the functional principles of the dog's structure remain the same. Unquestionably Judy O'Grady and the Colonel's Lady are sisters under the skin.

The perky Chihuahua has the identical number of bones and muscles, which he uses for the changeless principles of locomotion, as does the mighty Dane. This is true throughout dogdom despite the fact that some dogs are bred to meet specific and unusual conditions or to fit a pattern of fancy. The conformation that makes a crab-runner of a night hound will do the same for My Lady's Pom. The applied principles of movement and coordination of the various parts of the body are the same for all moving four-legged animals. The turn-spit dogs in the old English taverns did best with the angulation and conformation that suited the Belgian Maten pulling the milk carts of Flanders or the Percheron wheeling the hay in from the field.

Once we realize that the laws of moving and the fitting of parts together remain the same for all breeds, even unto the variations that dominate some, then our study into factors that lie behind our standards is simplified. To make the most of this, we must first know the foundation formula for each part and then the conformation of the whole. After that, we can apply our variations and understand the effect they have on other parts.

Again I repeat, it is that which lies behind a standard that is significant.

2
Dogs As We Have Made Them

THE Borzoi is a tall, dignified, complacent fellow that may not even look like a dog to the diminutive Yorkshire. These two and those others that fill the bracket between them may have had a little extra equipment added by the whims of fashion, the quirk of a judge or a clique, but in the main they were created by that architect who persists in fitting characteristics of the living into the requirements and place where the job is to be done.

Disregarding surface decorations, these animals became what they are because man had a little business for them to conduct, and he kept swapping around until he found the kind of dog that was best suited for it. And having done that he named it an "It dog." The history of every breed takes us back to the desires of man whether for work or decoration.

Those desires gave us a hound which could put a fox to-hole, and then a big-little dog which could get in the hole and bring the fox out. They gave us the Pointers and Setters with acute directional scenting ability and the hounds that run by ground trail. The desire of man developed the acute possessiveness of the shepherd types, as he persisted in breeding a good herd dog to a good herd dog. And the big sleeve of the Chinese Lords and Mandarins was father to the Pekingese.

A good example of how dogs were warped to man's desires can be found in Louisiana among the hog dogs of the Tensas swamp where hogs, which would not drive but charged instead, had to be corralled.

Over the vast unfenced timber lands of that section it is

profitable to range hogs in untended droves. Originally these were good Berkshires and other pure-bred animals like those fellows we see lolling lazily under the blue ribbons at fairs. Though their ancestors were recently sleepy-

Work afield designed a little-big dog to go in the hole after the varmint as it did a big dog to put the varmint there.

eyed prospects for pork chops, these denizens of the swamps are about the toughest brutes one wants to encounter, with tusks like ivory sabers. No animal reverts in ferocity more quickly than does the hog and there is none more deadly and determined in its attack. The bear and wolf of the Tensas step a wide circle around them and the dogs that corral them show the same respect.

"How in the world do you get them to market?" we asked Louie, a caretaker, who was acting as a guide on a duck shoot. "You say you can't drive them, that the whole drove turns on you."

"Oh, the dogs get 'em in the corral as easy as molasses spreads on a griddle cake."

"But don't they turn on the dogs?"

"Yeah, but that's the pigeon . . . say stick around during the week, we gotta make up a shipment and you can see how it's done."

A few mornings later we rode into the swamp on broad-hoofed ponies with three of Louie's dogs, an old bitch and two younger males. At first glance they were typical of those hounds one can find under almost any cotton picker's cabin in the South—dogs that take a trail with rolling tongue and run their prey to ground, tree or kill; lazy, but often deadly fighters.

Soon the old gyp started ranging out with casts reminiscent of a Setter working birds, but the two males still plodded at the horses' heels. We had been riding less than an hour when there came a loud squeal at the end of one of the gyp's casts and the males awoke from their slumber and dashed ahead in the direction of the commotion.

"She's got 'em!" Louie shouted as he urged his pony through the palmettos and tangled undergrowth.

At the scene of action there was a drove of hogs formed in battle array behind a lean-jawed boar bearing down on the gyp that had apparently been worrying a shoat which had wandered off to the side too far.

In the sunlight, the boar's tusks seemed better than six inches long though it was the leanness of his face that made them appear more deadly than those of domesticated hogs. You should thank the farmers for hiding such things under fat when you visit their stys.

As this array of white ivory bore down on the gyp, the other dogs charged with boisterous tongues from a different angle. The boar hesitated for but a split second and then swerved, the drove coming with him as a unit to meet the two male dogs.

The air was electric with the anticipation of a great fight, one that would put all others between dogs and wolves or bobcats down in the petty column. Even the trees seemed to hold their breath in expectancy.

Little more than ten feet seemed to separate these animals when the two dogs wheeled about as though spinning on an acorn and ran for their lives with every hog in mad pursuit. This show of cowardice came as a disappointing shock as though some trusted friend had suddenly dashed a bucket of cold water over you. I could scarcely keep a sneer off my face as I watched the hogs chase these dogs for some 300 or 400 yards, disappearing into the undergrowth, before the distinguishing sound of their slackened pace showed that they were abandoning the chase, feeling satisfied that they had rid themselves of these pests.

Almost instantly, I heard the dogs come back with bluster and I knew that the charge was on again, leaving me to wonder whether the dogs were fortunate enough to make their spin and get away in time. Now, following Louie as he pushed his pony in cautious pursuit, careful lest he draw the attack of the hogs away from the dogs, it gradually seeped into my mind what this was all about. By this constant heckling, the dogs would lead the hogs to the corral. Only one thing kept the repetition from becoming boresome,—I knew that the least slip in timing meant death.

The gyp had carefully circled the hogs at wide range and her high-pitched, sharp tongue could now be heard, like a dagger prick, prodding the hogs into another assault.

Eventually we arrived in sight of the corral; a long, narrow structure with high walls and two large gates standing open. The hogs were making their last attack into the enclosure as two men appeared from behind the wall to swing the gates closed.

"But the dogs!"

Louie chuckled as the three dogs came trotting around the corner with tongues out and that disinterested expression with which hounds view the rest of the world when they are not working game.

"There's a window at the far end of the corral, about three and a half feet off the ground—they jump through it."

"You taught them to —"

"Heck no—but if they don't learn, we don't bother with 'em any more."

The thought was disquieting. "But you have to train them for this work?"

HOW QUALITIES ARE PRODUCED

"Naw—you don't train a hog dog—you just breed 'em. Take a good natural hog dog and breed her to a good hog dog, that's all. Of course, some of the pups don't come out'n the swamp but them that does are hog dogs."

At first that method might leave a chill of cruelty creeping up our spine and then its simplicity somewhat salves the shock. Riding back, I could not miss the fact that it did give a rather true answer to the origin of all working breeds and, upon second thought, to non-workers and toys as well, to wit, the breeding of one individual which did a job well or had a certain desired feature to another equally well endowed.

When we reached Louie's home, a little boy came out to meet us, dragging a huge hound by its ear.

"That's a powerful looking animal."

"Him?" Louie sneered. "He's by Old Drive out of Nellie, two of the best dogs that ever worked on hogs, but that critter couldn't keep out'n a hog's way two minutes.

Never would have kept him 'cept the kid raised such a holler."

As the dog turned, his straight shoulders and unbent stifles were apparent. So this swampman was rejecting the same features that a judge in morning coat should turn down in a show ring. The swampman knew only by experience that a dog like him "couldn't keep out'n a hog's way two minutes." He did not know the reasons, he had never bothered to analyze them as the bench-show judge should do. However, unlike the latter's decision, if Louie had not discarded these features, the hogs would have.

In this, as in the history of the origin of the majority of breeds, it is evident that the correct feature was not a question of personal opinion in the beginning. Working results molded the basic principles and, unbelievable as it may seem, these are the same for all breeds.

The very wording of the original standards show that their authors were more interested in working features than in decorations. This same evidence points out that those men had sound knowledge of more animals than composed one breed of dogs; they were unquestionably good horsemen or they would not have crammed the standards with a multiplicity of horse terms. Diversified knowledge, and the ability to rationalize it, gives us a more complete understanding of the project ahead.

When the Fox Terrier Standard says: *He should stand like a cleverly made hunter,* it draws for the horseman a picture of an animal with the conformation adapted to taking the rough terrain in stride, but it means very little to one not acquainted with the structure of a "cleverly made hunter."

SOURCE OF DESCRIPTIVE TERMS

Hocks well let down, comes from the horse term, "hocks and knees well let down," and is synonymous with "hocks

The problems of any dog that goes afield, as well as the pack hound running to horse, are identical with those of horses covering the same ground. Note that each of the hounds is relatively in the same stride position as one of the horses. The problems encountered are even more trying on the dog than the horse because of difference in size.

and knees close to the ground." *Standing well up on hocks, well ribbed up,* and many other terms were taken from the paddock because they were used there long before one ever thought of a written standard for dogs.

The similarity of the horse and dog goes even further than these borrowed terms. This was emphasized by an instance at a Maryland show one year when two staunch Beagle fanciers talked at the ringside with a woman who had never shown any interest in dogs but who was a well known judge at horse shows.

"Have these boys finally got you interested in beagling?"

"Not in this generation," she replied. "These two simps have a bet on—Ed thinks I can judge dogs but I don't know one earthly thing about them."

"That's what she thinks," Ed said smugly as a press agent confident that his propaganda is so convincing that it will annoy the other side. "Here comes the first puppy class. It's time for you to get to work, young lady. Just forget that you are looking at dogs and judge these little animals as you did middle-weight hunters in Virginia last Saturday. Pick out the best middle-weight hunter you see in that ring."

The lady did; and it's a cinch that Ed won his bet. In fact, she missed only two first-place dogs on the entire Beagle program.

Why should that not be true? Beagles working afield have the same locomotive problems to solve as do middle-weight hunters. Though woven of the same fabric, the little cotton-tail chaser finds his ground even more taxing than does the horse, because what to the latter is a mere gully, to the former becomes a chasm.

If the Thoroughbred hunter has found a conformation that traverses rough ground to the best advantage, then this same conformation can be applied to dogs which meet similar problems afield. Which of the horse types

we pick as patterns will depend on whether we seek speed
or endurance, and over what type of ground the dog must
work. We have a good illustration of this in the Foxhounds which vary from the long legged, short bodied,
relatively light-weight animals to the sturdier so-called
English Foxhound; they each meet some working condition better.

Many of the old breeders took pointers from horse

Little old ladies with white bonnets and dogs pulling milk carts
are as much a part of Belgian towns as the towers and bells.
Perhaps more dogs are yet used for draft in Belgium than horses.

types in producing their animals, whether hounds, terriers or other field dogs. Even at this writing in Belgium where as many dogs are used for draft as horses, the Belgian Maten shows the same breeding choice as marks the great draft horses that take their name from this country.

The ancients who developed the gazehounds also took into consideration the features that did a job well for other animals and applied them to their dogs. In that way we got the double-suspension gallop which matched that of the prey their dogs pursued. But like the Bedouin Chieftains, who developed the great Nejdee horse in the fifth century, they have not improved on the original development in 1400 years.

A little more of that conformation which enables a cheetah to spot a Greyhound twenty yards and pass him in 400 would certainly help the Greyhound win a few sheckles on a Florida dog track. "But," a modern dog breeder grumbles, "who has the time or chance to study the conformation of the cheetah?"

"And as for that," a friend put in, "my Afghan might help me catch a blonde in a rabbit coat but not by coursing her through Central Park. His job for me is to attract attention and start conversations."

A CONSIDERATION OF OTHER BREEDS

It has always been difficult to get the "modern" breeder of any specific variety of dog to give consideration to other varieties and especially other species of animals beyond that of his own choice. A national dog magazine ran a series of articles pertaining to all breeds, and a check showed that Doberman breeders read those illustrated by that dog while Shepherd breeders rather confined themselves to the ones illustrated by Shepherds.

"Why should I worry about how a horse gallops," said a lady in a two-point sweater with a handful of Toy

Manchester, "unless I've got a two-dollar ticket on him? But," she continued, "tell me how I can get better fronts on my dogs."

This lady reminded us of the child fingering a half-finished model as he asked, "Dad, what makes an airplane fly?"

"Well, son," the father started then hesitated, stumped as to how far to go in his explanation, "it is kept aloft by—" but then he was saved the trouble, another kid had called from the front gate and the boy was gone. He really did not want an answer to his question.

There is still more analogy between the lady and the boy, between breeding dogs and making airplane models. Give the same type model planes to two boys—one who has a fair understanding of dihedral, drag, incidence, balance and other factors, while the other has asked for the information and skipped off to play at another game—and see which of the two hand you back the best assembly. Had we given the lady the answer to her question about improving fronts, it is likely she would find it too much trouble to follow. Besides she has promised to breed to Mrs. Brown's new champion.

It does not make much difference where the dog came from—the Garden of Eden, Noah's Ark, a fish that wiggled ashore and borrowed four legs from somebody's imagination or the long extinct ancestor of the wolf and coyote—they have been molded into gadgets for us to use, admire or play with, afield or on a cushion. As a hundred-odd varieties parade by, we might marvel at the changes we have wrought and yet, if we will but take the second look, we find the variation is only superficial. Even today they are basically the same as those whose fossils we find with the bones of our club courting ancestors.

We cannot put them together with the preciseness of a model airplane whether it is to decorate a shelf or do a little sailing, but we do have to produce something that works. "Work" in this sense does not mean digging ditches, finding birds or shaking rats; it is like a clock ticking or a jig-saw puzzle fitting together without missing or contorted parts.

If we want an ornament, there is no reason why we should not have one. If we want a field dog or just something that our neighbor does not have, it is our privilege.

Whether a pet or field dog, conformation must be functional as well as adherent to the characteristic pattern of the breed.

Yet the clock has to tick; the structural and working parts, whether for toy or giant, must fit together and work in a manner that is the least tiring, most graceful and efficient in movement. These parts, unassembled, can be blueprinted and studied for mechanical efficiency. Which study should give us a clearer understanding of the part and its relation to the components! We cannot recognize the weak points unless we know what makes them weak, and what mechanical change might compensate for or correct them.

Though we cannot put the dog together like we do a bridge, we have put him together by our choice of his ancestors and made him big or little, long or short, fluffy or wire-haired, and sometimes we have not been too wise in our selection of parts. Our domestic animals are handicapped by the fact that we force the parts upon them and preserve the bad along with the good. The animals of the wild, as complete species, have been more fortunate because of that great selection process known as the survival of the fittest.

When our ancestors first developed the breed with which we fell in love, they had experience afield to guide them so that they could cull the efficient performers from the ones that did not do so well. This accounts for the quality that has been handed to us in our dogs. In the main we lack the experience or even the opportunity to observe performance so that we can measure the advantages of features and maintain the quality which has been given us.

Our only recourse, then, is to figure out what the part does, how it works and what makes the difference between the good and the bad, or more specifically what is good and what is bad. Maybe such a study does loom as tiresomely academic but so were the bridge and golf lessons that took us out of the dud class. Just as it is more pleasure to play any game well, you will likely find it more fun breeding dogs as they should be, to function efficiently, as to take a chance on uncertain luck. Besides that is one way to have something that your neighbor does not possess.

3

Conformation

W E MIGHT paraphrase the difference between Madame and Mademoiselle, which of course is Monsieur, by pointing out that the distinction between a good and bad specimen in the canine world is conformation. That, however, is a term we have heard slapped all over the show rings like a cocktail shaker at a summer party, and like the contents of the shaker it offers a mixture of uncertainties.

It is true that words do became cloaked in special robes for various fields of activity, the new version seemingly unakin to the original roots. However, upon examination we find a basic connection that justifies the application and, what is more to the point, it is standardized. We feel safe in saying that those who first used the terms *conformation* and *angulation* were not trying to coin colloquialisms but had in mind their fundamental meanings.

"Conformation," says the dictionary, "is conformity, adaptation; the shaping of a thing by orderly arrangement of its parts." By its very meaning, that does force two considerations on us when applying it to dogs in general. It must follow the specified pattern of the breed to which it is being applied, and a dog can do it while remaining in a show-ring posture though never moving. Adaptation even suggests a modification of the structure which enables it to conform advantageously to the pattern.

Our second consideration must be its functional possibilities, for the dog cannot always stand poised in a show-ring posture. The arrangement of parts, by necessity of movement, must be such that the pattern is efficient in

26

operation. This applies to all breeds from the largest to the smallest.

Thus we do find that we have stationary or *static* conformation, and functional or *kinetic* conformation. Maybe the two can be separated but this usually results in a loss to one with the glorification of the other. The picture created by both must remain constant; therefore, they have to be one and the same.

Unfortunately many of the finished patterns to which the various breeds should adhere have been tossed in the same category as the old farmer did the weather when he remarked: "Time was when a man could judge it but since the government's took it over you never know what they are going to do with it." Even when cliques and fanciers deal out new pictures, we can cut the tail off to conform with them but we cannot cast aside the body or the running gear.

A Bulldog without a hide and a half is no more Bulldog than a hinny is a mule in the stockman's eye, but the scowl was originally unintentional and a by-product of a functional goal to which the original breeders aimed and even now does not eliminate the dog's means of transportation. Therefore we must consider *conformation* as not only fitting a specific picture but as making that picture work efficiently.

Angulation must come into consideration and this, according to the dictionary, applies to the angles formed by lines and planes; in the dog's case, of his body and working parts. Generally it is used to refer to the angles created by the bones of the forehand and rearhand assemblies within themselves and with the plane on which the dog stands in normal posture. Specifically it is the degree with which these angles and lines conform to the desired pattern of the whole.

Fitting, or the adaptation of one part to another, is even more important than the make-up of the individual part, for it is only in this manner that a practical mechanism can be created. Like the ciphers in arithmetic, counting for little when standing alone, conformation of part to part gives the final value to the integral number.

Several years ago, Matt, an old field trialer, was chiding a bench-show judge. The latter had just put up a Pointer handled by a girl, whose dress fit her as though it liked the job, over another with a fair trial record behind him.

"Ah, the girl had nothing to do with it," the judge defended with a blush. "Her dog was much better angulated behind though, I'll have to admit, he wasn't nearly as good in front."

"And that," Matt charged, "was the very best reason for reversing your decision. The dog you put up had too much angulation behind for what his shoulders would stand. I've seen too many of your dogs with excellent angulation behind and none to speak of in front soon lost by brace-mates that were just fair on both ends."

It is true that two mediocre units which conform concisely to one another will produce better results under working conditions than if one is of such superior quality as to break up the conformity. That is the real keynote of conformation as it applies to action or locomotion.

We can illustrate this by assuming that a dog has hindquarters with 60-pound drive and forequarters capable of absorbing only 40 pounds, and then compare its potential action with one rated at 45 pounds, fore and aft. The former, like the cat, will have more initial speed but lose to the latter when endurance enters the game.

It is this unbalance of driving and receiving conformation which is primarily responsible for the majority of race horses breaking down in front; it is the reason why more bad fronts develop on the sprinters than on the distance horses. You are not interested in horses but you can take a lesson from them. In fact, you can take lessons from every animal of the wild, for every one that moves afield can teach you something about functional conformation.

Animals of the wild have been bred and developed to meet their specific conditions of life by the greatest selectionist operating—the survival of the fittest. These babies are good within their scope because they have to be good to stay there. Many of them fail under certain tests and pass out of the picture, and in this passing we

Every animal that moves afield can teach us something about functional conformation.

can find the reasons, usually in lack of initial speed or failure to maintain it.

The mountain lion, for instance, dines on horse flesh only by stealth or the first quick sweep of attack. If he does not get the horse immediately—and he is quite afraid of those hoofs—he just does not eat horse today. One has the conformation for quick initial spring,—the lion may cover better than 25 feet in his first leap—the other, to keep right on going once he gets started. It is not difficult to determine the features that mark the difference and profit by them in selecting our dogs for breeding regardless of which feature we wish to emphasize.

All animals—and dogs are no exception—have a tendency to adjust themselves to lack of conformation in their running gear. However, domestic animals have to do more of this than those of the wild. The dog that "crabs" or "pads" is making such an adjustment, and any show ring will reveal a sizable number of them.

COMPOSITION AND MAKE-UP

Later we will stress stationary or static, and functional or kinetic balance, and point out that never the twain should part or be forgotten. In some of our sporting breeds, we have examples wherein they did part, perhaps never to meet again. In this lies a compensating factor in the human make-up; those dogs which streak across the fields to trial wins may look like the country cousins of the ones strutting to victory in the show ring, but the field trialer sees them as a thing of beauty and puts the others down as lap dogs.

We are somewhat inclined to see more foundation *for* the trialer's opinion than *against* it, for the dog which wins the big-time stakes or those which bring home the heavy tin from behind electric rabbits must have balance. The artist, or anyone with an eye for composition and make-up, will always appreciate the beauty in symmetry and balance.

No one would expect every dog to be a champion in the field or on the track. Few of them are bred for that purpose; likewise they are not bred for powder puffs and lap warmers. We may hold the Chihuahua in our hands to

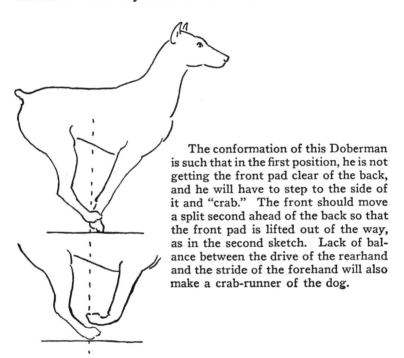

The conformation of this Doberman is such that in the first position, he is not getting the front pad clear of the back, and he will have to step to the side of it and "crab." The front should move a split second ahead of the back so that the front pad is lifted out of the way, as in the second sketch. Lack of balance between the drive of the rearhand and the stride of the forehand will also make a crab-runner of the dog.

get a closer view of that expressive little face but the rascal is far more interesting when he chases his shadow on the rug. Then again, even in the show ring, we are judging the animal on perfection, the fitting to a pattern which has four legs as a part of it: those four legs must harmonize with each other and the thing to which they are attached in a manner approaching perfection else we prefix a little "imp" for imperfection.

One of the first places in which lack of harmony shows

up is in the gait either by padding, pounding, crabbing or short, stilted action to avoid interference between front and back legs.

The normal gait is so timed that the front leg moves a split-second ahead of the back leg. This should let the pad of the front be lifted and get out of the way of the back pad. The longer the stride and the faster the gait, the more necessary this action becomes. If the body is too short, the stride too long, or the timing not just right, the dog will have to sidestep and run like a crab.

The coupling comes into this consideration and is, in itself, a relative thing. The length of a dog's body is the distance from the tip of the sternum to the tip of the buttock. To take this accurately, it should be done with a special measuring stick provided with a fixed squared arm at one end and a sliding squared arm on the stick. The measurement should be on a line parallel to the center line of the body. Coupling is the distance between the front assembly and the back assembly.

A dog may have a long body but, with well-laid-back shoulders and acutely angulated hindquarters, appear short coupled because the distance between the two assemblies is relatively short in comparison with the whole body. A deep body, regardless of other features, tends to make the dog appear short coupled. Shallow bodies therefore make the dog look as though long coupled.

A long coupled dog will usually have upright shoulders and straight stifles with a short croup and possibly a shallow body. However, many of the good racing Greyhounds have long couplings with none of these faults solely because they have extremely long bodies. Dogs like Dachshunds are also long in coupling without the faults designated as a rule by the condition, unless they are long by comparison with well proportioned, long bodied dogs.

MEASUREMENTS ARE RELATIVE

You will find that the majority of these features are all relative. They can be judged in no other manner. That which is "short" for one breed, or even one individual, may be long for another. You must consider the representative pattern of the breed and the purpose or intent of the given feature being examined and then project it against the whole.

Sometimes these comparisons can be made to better advantage against other animals. The Fox Terrier Standard uses several hundred words to give us a specific picture, yet in one statement—*stand like a cleverly made hunter*—tells us a volume about the conformation desired, that conformation which enables an Irish hunter to take the rough ground and jump in stride.

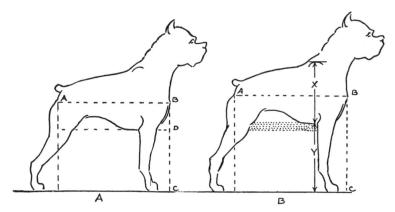

The amount of ground a dog covers is governed by the ratio of the sides of a rectangle formed by body length and a fixed-height point; the sternum (B) or the brisket (D) may be used for the latter. AB bears a greater ratio to BC in Dog A than in Dog B, therefore the former covers the most ground though similar in other features. Dog B, in this case is also leggy because line Y exceeds line X. He also shows too much daylight, the excess being shown by the shaded area. These are all relative factors, arrived at by comparison.

In the same manner, we must judge such applications as "cover ground." This is primarily the comparison of the distance from the dog's brisket or lower body line with that between the front and back assemblies. The daylight seen under the dog can be considered as a rectangle, and the comparison of the long side with the short side reveals the "amount of ground covered."

You can take any given dog, shorten its legs one inch and it will cover more ground than before the operation. Lengthening the legs will reduce the amount of ground covered. A long body adds to the ground covered, so sometimes will a long coupling, and bring with it the possible accompanying faults.

So often we have had dogs pointed out as being too long or short in neck or head, excessively high on the leg or any one of the many faults or virtues established by measurements, only to find that when these features are actually checked they are not what we thought.

Here is a dog which seems to have an extremely long head, yet it isn't, for it is the shortness of his neck or the cloddy or cobby build that makes the head appear long by comparison. Usually this optical illusion is created by something close to the feature in question. But you will always have to go beyond any single feature before you can feel certain that you have seen it right. For instance, is the dog short coupled or just a little too high on the leg? Is he really deep in body or slightly short of leg? Is it the neck and head length that is giving him the apparently compact body?

Those are questions of related measurements and must be considered as such. It is not practical to take them to the fraction of an inch. Better far to use the method of the artist with the objects before him which he intends to paint. This can be done easily from the ringside or any convenient distance from the dog when he is stationary. Hold a pencil or any small measuring stick at arm's length and eye level. Close one eye as you project this measure over the part of the dog chosen for checking or use in comparison with other parts. You can mark the length from the tip of the measure with your thumb nail. Strips of white cardboard can be used and dented with the

Though the heads of these Fox Terriers are the same size, the one to the left is relatively larger and therefore a "bigger head." A head may appear large because the neck is short or thin, the dog himself may be small; and so it is with all other features, they must be judged in their relation to one another.

thumb nail; the contrasting proportions can then be recorded and observed at leisure.

This is simply a means of determining ratio of parts or related lengths. For instance, the distance from elbow to withers can be compared with that of elbow to ground, total height checked against body length, or the head can be taken as a unit to judge the general proportions of the dog. Though this is not accurate to the fraction of an inch, by practice you can make it nearly so. The measurements taken on one dog cannot be projected on another unless you stand the same distance from each of them.

THE DOG IS DESIGNED BY WORK

You cannot find the conclusive answer by this or any other means without considering the intent as well as the influence or compensating factors of other features involved. The purpose for which the animal was created must always be before you as the background against which you examine the dog.

The Bulldog may be a house pet today but the keynotes of the screen against which you judge him are: low center of gravity, broad base of support, strength of jaw grip, with hide enough to roll himself out of it if he happened to be pinned under the bull.

The Sealyham and other low-set terriers were designed to go to ground through small holes and openings in the cairns to battle a fox, groundhog or other animal, and these must have free front leg action for digging, good bites, weather resistant coats, and agility.

While these two incidences show why we must take the origin and intent of the breed into consideration before judging the conformation, the wide variety of types found in the breed which can be blanketed under the name of Foxhound are even better examples. These hounds run fox and coon through the mountains of Kentucky, Tennessee or Virginia, while their counterparts trail fox, bobcats and wolves over the wide areas but less rugged sections of Oklahoma and Texas. It is easy to see why the one working the mountains has to be more agile afoot and possibly can do with less speed on the open run than those used in the West. Therefore the conformations are not identical, nor do either jibe up with the heavier, pack-running hound that works ahead of horses. The latter dogs more closely resemble the heavyweight hunter by comparison.

The specific purpose or aim of the animal should always prescribe the overall pattern and likewise the individual features that are put together to make this pattern. Unquestionably the conformation of the complete animal is the main concept, but as this is made up of individual parts, the parts must be examined for their ability to function. For instance, in horses and the majority of dogs, a request is made for "hocks well let down," which means that hock bones (metatarsus) are relatively short in comparison with other bones of the back legs. This is a definite gesture to sacrifice initial speed and take on a little more endurance.

The rabbit has exceptionally long hock bones and gets away with an initial leap often six times its extended body and leg length but lands in the coyote's dinner pail because it cannot maintain the speed. The cheetah and pronghorn are also long in hock but have some compensating factor that gives them endurance, particularly the latter. The meaning of this request is not to change the general structure but to improve it slightly in one feature.

If you had two rabbits identical in all other features except hock length, the longer one would "get away" first while the other would make more strides over a given distance but could hold its speed to better advantage. The rabbit, though, depends on its initial speed for its safety and therefore those that have survived are relatively long in hock.

The keynote of changing any individual feature is to secure better conformation with the whole, and particularly as regards the purpose of the animal.

In discussing these features, it may appear that we are more interested in the dogs that take us afield after game than in those that keep us company by the home fires. This is not the case; however, field workers furnish better examples of the same features which should be part of our Bostons, Manchesters or any breed not necessarily used in sport.

Seeking or trying to produce the ideal specimen of any

breed is like trying to find the illusive leprechaun. These little scamps, according to Irish legend, keep a pot of gold hidden in the woods for the sole purpose of paying ransom when they are caught. Catching one will end your financial troubles. They are green and only about nine inches tall, do not scratch or bite, but—and therein lies the trouble.

With dogs, though, we have a better chance than chasing little green dwarfs through brush and leaves, for we can study the cause and effect of the various features that we are trying to meld into the ideal. With that in mind we shall proceed to analyse what the dog does when he moves, and what the parts do to produce that movement and give him a conformation that is functional and not static.

4

The Dog's Slow Gaits

NO MATTER how sentimentally we may choose to catalogue him, the dog is the servant of mankind. He is
either a sporting agent, a companion, a means of liveli-
hood, a child's playmate, a worker in war or peace, and
perhaps a combination of these and other things. He
might be an outlet for thwarted mother complex, a salve
to our ego or merely a decoration for the lawn. In all of
which, though our feelings range from selfishness to sin-
cerity, he is our servant.

The first requisite of his service is that he must be alive,
for little pleasure can be derived from a dead dog. The
next is that he must move. Movement, which reduces
itself to gait, is the prime agent governing the result of
his service. The greatest trail-running nose in the world
would be of little good should the dog not be able to carry
it afield. The most lovable house pet becomes a burden
when its legs stop working.

Fancy may dictate that a few breeds be judged on
some specific feature such as head or coat almost to the
exclusion of other parts of the dog, but still he must move.
Fancy might shift with the ideas of a new clique, but the
dog moves on. Again in stationary outline, the dog might
be wonderful; in motion, a clumsy ox. The Dane on the
lawn may be stately as a bronze statue until he starts
lumbering across the turf. It has been said, and perhaps
rightly so, that if a dog moves right, he must be right.

So, the dog must move and movement brings us to *gaits*
or the various sequences which the legs follow in producing locomotion. It was not until we had the motion

picture camera that we had any real conception about these sequences. Down through the years there has been perpetual misconception of these facts and even now we find them lingering in the minds of many.

The owner of six fair thoroughbreds then racing at

Even the house pet finds it expedient to make tracks at times. In fact, every dog must move and movement brings us right up to the study of gaits.

Pimlico sat in a sportsman's bar going over some advertising sketches which had been made for his product, with horses as the main theme.

"They are nice pictures," he said, "but a horse does not run like this one."

Paradoxically, the walls of the bar were covered with racing photographs of which more than half showed horses with exactly or almost identical leg position. That he had never noticed this fact is not unusual even for one dealing in the field.

In the latter part of the nineteenth century, still cameras began to shed some light on what the legs did when moving the animal. Prior to that time, artists and veterinary books depicted gaits with leg action in impossible positions. It is a rare thing to find a horse or dog galloping correctly in an old print.

Even the other day, we came upon a recent drawing of a famous match trotter by a modern artist of national reputation—the horse was trotting with the off legs and pacing with the near ones. A publisher of dog literature used extensively a cut of a Fox Terrier that was pacing instead of trotting, its correct gait. This may be artistic license but is more likely habitual misconception or lack of applied thought.

All dogs walk, trot and, at times, pace or amble, as the gait is often called. Also they use three forms of the gallop: the canter and suspension gallop, each identical with the horse's sequence, and the leaping style employed by the cheetah, antelope and Indian buck. Before discussing these gaits in detail, we should get together on the terms used to describe various characteristics.

The *stride* is the distance from one ground mark to the next made by the same pad.

Suspension is the time during which all legs are off the ground and the dog is being propelled by sheer momentum.

Timing or *time* refers to the number of changes which take place in the support of the body by the legs. If two legs support the body and then transfer the job directly to the other pair, the gait is *two-time*. Three distinct changes in the support produce a *three-time* gait; four distinct changes, a *four-time* gait.

Right diagonal and *left diagonal* are terms used to describe the support when it is by one front foot and the opposite back foot. The right or left front foot determines which diagonal is being employed.

Sequence is the complete action of all four legs.

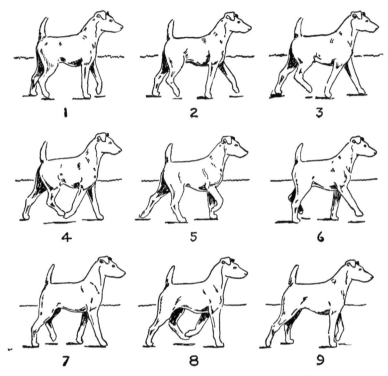

THE WALK—In the nine diagrams, the Fox Terrier dem' onstrates the complete sequence of a full stride of the walk The left front starts the action. Positions 1 and 2 show the right diagonal; 3, right diagonal and left front; 4, the left lateral; 5 and 6, the left diagonal; 7, the left diagonal and right front; 8, the right lateral; and 9 takes us back to the start.

THE WALK

The walk is a four-time movement, in which all legs move one after another, setting up four different combinations of weight support. At least two if not three legs aid the support at all times. For this reason the gait is the least tiring of any and is almost invariably employed by the animal for leisure travel.

The dog rarely begins to walk with the back foot but prefers to lead off with the front. The mechanical reason for this is that if the front acts a split-second ahead of the back it is more apt to clear the way for the back and not cause interference, forcing the dog to side-step.

When the dog starts or leads off with the left front foot, it is followed by the right rear, then the right front and left rear. The gait takes advantage of both diagonals in this sequence. As the left front has moved first, it is advanced and implanted so that it can take over the front support and allow the right front to be lifted out of the way of the advancing back foot in time to prevent the two hitting. Each foot is in motion for about half the time required for the complete sequence and therefore bears weight for the other half. Should the dog start with the right front, the sequence remains the same, for the left rear comes into play next.

There are three types of walk, characterized by the length of stride. Two factors enter into producing these: conformation of the angulation of the fore and rear hand assemblies, and neurotic reflexes.

The short striding or power walk is suitable to those dogs which draw a pay load such as the sledges of the North country and the milk carts of Europe. It was also valuable to the turn-spit dogs of old England. The animal most adapted to it is characterized by being stocky, heavy, low-set with strong shoulders and hips, short muscular legs, short neck less erect than other dogs'. The side supports should never act quite unaided by one or more of the opposite supports, for more pull is registered when the diagonals come into play.

Two types of shoulders seem adaptable to this class and give rather similar results. One has a well-laid-back blade with a shorter, more upright upper arm, still retaining 90 degrees between the two. This shoulder is found on any good draft horse. The other has an almost upright shoulder blade and an upper arm that sets nearly parallel to the ground when not in motion, and is characteristic of draft oxen. The draft horse and the ox, as well as all dogs following this pattern, need not be as acutely angulated as those that use the normal or fast striding walk.

In judging draft horses they stress form, quality and hocks first, and then the croup and gaskins before considering other factors. This order should apply equally to the dog which is to be used for draft or which must employ power in the same manner. When making his kill of a rodent, the terrier applies power into the push which he gives with the same muscles as those used by the ox and horse for pulling.

The normal walk has a stride which just about covers the front pad mark with the rear. While less need be said to distinguish this from the other styles, it is characteristic of and adapted to better than 80 per cent of the breeds.

The stride in any breed will be shortened by long couplings, short legs, not standing well up on hocks, straight stifles, flat croup, soft muscles and poor condition. Therefore without looking for these features or faults in any given dog, a comparatively short stride prognosticates them where the stride should be normal.

An over-reach of the back pad mark beyond the front indicates short coupling, stiltedness and straight shoulder blades coupled with a rearhand too well angulated for the forehand.

The long striding walk does produce an over-reach unless the animal has a comparatively long body or short legs. In other animals, the greatest exponent of this style is the Tennessee Walking Horse, which was developed in the South for use by overseers on large plantations.

Some may contend, and rightly so, that this is not a true walk but is, like the fox trot, a transitional pace between the walk and trot. It is not often encountered in dogs but is used by some German Shepherd Dogs and others possessing acute angulation in both front and rear assemblies.

In the walk, as in all gaits, the heel pads strike the ground first and therefore receive the first impact of the weight and force; the toes come into play only for leverage action after the pad has become set. For that reason, heel pads should be well filled in and of good quality to absorb the shock and withstand the abrasion of ground contact.

THE TROT

"I have never seen much sense in trotting dogs in a show ring," said a field trial fan. "My Pointers had better not waste time trotting at a field trial."

"You trot and like it," grumbled a Whippet owner puzzled as to what the trot reveals of his little bang-tail's ability to streak around the oval.

Another companion pointed to a girl who snapped shut-eyes open. "Maybe she doesn't have anything that other girls don't but she certainly shows it to better advantage. It's the same with the trot. It shows the faults and virtues of a dog's running gear more clearly to the judge than any other gait regardless of whether he's a galloper by trade or not."

The trot is a two-time gait and the simplest of all. Its sequence is just one diagonal after the other, the left front and right rear legs moving in unison with each other as do the right front and left rear. Except in the flying trot, which has a period of suspension, the body always has support. To insure this perpetual support, the front foot moves slightly in advance of its coordinating back foot which gets it clear of the approaching back lateral. The more distinct this characteristic is, up to a certain point, the smoother will be the gait.

"Smooth—my aching seat!" says a novice rider as he sips his drink by the club-room mantel.

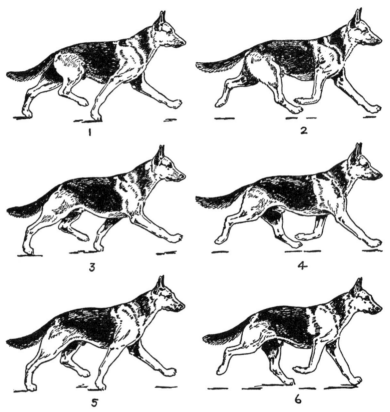

THE TROT—This German Shepherd in positions 1 and 3 shows the right and left diagonal, the two supports of the trot. Positions 2 and 4 show suspension which follows each diagonal in the "flying trot," which is rarely seen unless the dog is specifically bred for it. For the long stride as shown the dog must have excess body length over height to avoid the front and back leg hitting. THE PACE—Positions 5 and 6 show the right and left lateral of the pace, which is a fatigue gait and has never been highly developed in dogs. It must offer a restful change for dogs resort to it after a hard day's work.

The bouncing rider is caught between the conflict of the two diagonals, the posting rider goes with that force. Poor conformation and upright shoulders make the gait rougher to both rider and animal. All gaits produce a shock to the front assembly, but if a trotter's shoulders are correctly placed, this shock passes through them with a minimum effect, being absorbed by the muscles, and there is less rise and fall to the withers and back line, which should be apparent to the eye and tell the judge a story.

This shock is ever present in the dog's trot. Some are so constructed as to absorb the most of it while others manifest it quite plainly. Watch a pack of hounds jogging down the road and you can pick out the good fronts almost invariably just by watching the withers. You can do the same thing with dogs in the show ring. Take your eyes off flashing legs for a moment and note the action of the withers. Then make yourself a mental bet on the dog whose withers move along with least bounce.

The Standardbred horse is the best of our domestic trotters where speed is concerned. The Thoroughbred, particularly the type selected for Remount, runs him a close second. A little study of the conformation that makes this possible should benefit dog breeders. It may be difficult to rationalize the work of a Chihuahua or field trial Setter with that of a trotting horse but it should not require a second thought to realize that the factors producing this smoothness, speed and endurance will also contribute to gracefulness, lack of effort and general proficiency of the dog's gait.

Size for size, the coyote is perhaps the greatest trotter among wild animals even though the fox is a skilful performer. The coyote has been known to cruise between 15 and 20 miles within an hour, using the trot exclusively.

The most dexterous of the wild animals at the trot is the moose. This big fellow has been timed over distances of 15 and 20 miles down river beds and over rough ground at rates as high as 2:10 per mile. It is a very rare thing that he ever gallops and when we compare this time with the speed of our best horses over prepared tracks we can appreciate his proficiency, the secret of which is likely his superb shoulders.

In comparing the value of the trot with the gallop as a means of locomotion our judgement may be warped by the memory of some of our great flat track racers. Yet, when we consider that the best running time for the mile is only about 20 seconds faster than for the trotter pulling a sulky, it gives us a different slant. What is more, the trotter is often asked to work five 1-mile heats in an afternoon to win a single race while the galloper usually gets a week or more rest and training between races. It is that ability to keep on going which gives the trot its value. What applies to horses in this applies equally to dogs.

The trot is admirably suited for rough, irregular ground and for traveling long distances at a fair rate of speed. It is the natural foraging gait of most wild animals. No one leg has more work to do that its opposite and the diagonal support makes it easier for the dog to maintain equilibrium.

THE FLYING TROT

The flying trot which the Standardbred horse uses on the track has a period of suspension between each diagonal. The German Shepherd Dog has been developed until this double suspension is characteristic of his gait. It is not the result of being lifted high into the air but by the momentum of the drive shooting the dog through the air while the legs are all partly contracted in the natural sequence.

It is usually said of match trotters that they are "no better than their boots," the protective pads fastened to their front legs to prevent the back hoofs clipping and cutting them by the long stride. It is not practical to put boots on our dogs so we must prevent clipping by some other means. This can be done by either shortening the legs or lengthening the body. Shepherd breeders are producing a long body with a low center of gravity which eliminates this interference and is the most practical way that dog breeders can secure the sweep of the flying trot without clipping or crab-running.

The long body in the German Shepherd was not accomplished by its breeders until after 1930, except in a few scattered specimens. They were putting acute angulation in the back legs and getting a tremendous drive that resulted in numerous side-wheelers or crab runners. Once they abandon or neglect the ratio of body length to height, the dog will revert to one of two things: a crab runner or the normal stride of the shorter bodied animal.

For this flying trot to be functioning correctly, the dog's back line gets closer to the ground as though he is slightly crouched, the withers maintain a level course and the back legs seem to be digging in and throwing the ground behind them. Top speed is not the general idea but overall perfection of movement, which in itself produces speed; this is the goal.

There is a vast difference between a long body and a long coupling. An example is the great Rysdak's Hambletonian, the progenitor of at least 70 per cent of all match trotters which have clipped the 2:30 mark since his son, George Wilkes, trotted 2:24¾ at the Fashion course on Long Island in 1862. Old Ham was extremely long in coupling but not one single descendant which resembled him in this respect was ever successful at the stud or on the track. His fast progeny were short coupled though some had long bodies.

It can rightly be said that to the observer the trot will reveal the structure and conformation of the dog more than any other gait—it is a window that shows you the entire room.

"Paces," the ringside observer jots opposite a dog's name in a show catalogue and you can almost see the sneer in the pencil marks. Perhaps that should be, yet the gait does not deserve all the ridicule it has received. Its appearance can tell us a lot about the individual dog provided we know the significance.

THE PACE

In some fields the pace is referred to as the amble. It is a two-time, lateral gait. That is, the left front and left back legs move in unison, while the two right legs do likewise. The body weight is carried first by one pair of laterals and is then shifted to the other pair. In the pace, the front leg also moves a split-second ahead of its coordinating back leg to give better support and to aid the other laterals.

Propulsion is relatively along the line of progress which results in less lateral deviation. Equilibrium is not quite as easily maintained as in the trot but the gait is relatively free of fatigue generators.

Napoleon preferred pacers to all other gaited horses for long marches and he certainly had ample chance to make a study of them. The natives of Iceland and Dutch South Africa persist in breeding them for both working and riding. If the timing is such that the cross-support enters into it, the gait is smooth with very little rise and fall to the withers and back line.

Years ago the harness racing fancy condemned the pacer as positively as do dog breeders the same gait; but the horseman could not keep the pacer in the dark by making light of him. As persistently as the dandelions on our front lawn, he popped up and demanded attention. At first the pacer was permitted to race with the trotter but that short story too often ended with the trotter on the short end of the purse. Then they made special races for the pacer; it is slightly faster.

Two facts stand out in this transition: The pace proved the faster of the two gaits and famous trotters, as they grew old, suddenly emerged even better pacers, not by the owner's choice but the horse's. Therein lies a square meal of thought for the dog breeder.

For one thing, evidence marks this out as a fatigue gait, or a product of physical weakness. Foals and puppies often pace before they learn to trot, taking to the latter only after their muscles develop and become firm. So when the over-fat and out-of-condition dogs resort to it, the gait is but pointing the finger of accusation at the dog's condition.

The match trotter turned to it when he became footsore and leg-weary either from age or overwork. It is not unusual to see a great going field trial dog display a sound, level gallop throughout competition and then come ambling up to the cars on the gallery hill, or hounds which have finished a hard run on a fox's trail shuffling down the road in a disgraceful pace. There must be some reason why animals turn to it when tired or out of condition.

Interference is perhaps another agent that makes a pacer out of a dog. Over angulated behind for conformation and balance with the forehand, he finds it easier to exchange the diagonals of the trot with their constant clipping for the greater foot freedom of the laterals instead of continuing to run crab-wise.

Beneath all this there is perhaps one underlying factor which brings out this gait at such times; it is the animal's reluctance to fight *lateral displacement,* an ever present force in all gaits which is recognized by many horsemen but by few dog breeders. This force should be given serious consideration in studying all gaits for it is constantly trying to slap the good mover for a loop.

Even though the pace is a restful gait to which the tired dog resorts after a hard day's work, there is no vindication for the show ring competitor using it and the spectator was justified in putting a sneer in the pencil marks of the catalogue notation.

5

The Dog's Fast Gaits

A RUG goes skidding as a Toy Manchester scampers across the room . . . a Boston Terrier tied to a bouncing ball . . . through snow tipped brush a cottontail leads a Beagle . . . beneath a new moon resting lazily in the pine trees, a hound unlimbers on a coon's trail . . . into the wind, head high, streak two Pointers—all of them galloping. It is a natural gait for all dogs and is utilized by them in one of its three forms either in play or service to the owner.

The style of a Pointer or Setter going afield depends upon the character of his gallop; the speed of a Whippet, the grace of a Collie or Dane, the agility of a Terrier are hallmarked by the letter of their gallop.

The three distinct styles of this gait used by dogs are: the *sustained,* which horsemen call the "canter;" the *normal,* which is identical with that of the running horse; the *leaping,* similar to the antelope, cheetah and Indian buck's specialty.

When cruising or loping easily across the field or yard, the dog prefers the sustained because it is less tiring and gives better support for body weight. It is by no means as fast as the others, often being much slower than the trot, but it can be shifted into the fast normal gallop with no more effort than a tail wag. The distribution of support makes it ideal for rough ground or where footing is uncertain.

THE CANTER

It is a three-time gait in which the specific supports are *right rear, right diagonal,* and *left front* when leading to the left; or left rear, left diagonal, and right front when leading to the right. The front leg which is not a part of the diagonal is called the "leading leg" and the dog is said to "lead to the right" or "lead to the left." While these changes are taking place, each support receives some aid from the one just passing or the one coming into play which is a distinct benefit to it along the endurance line.

The leading leg is a major consideration in both this and the normal gallop, for it bears weight for a longer period than either of the other supports and over it the dog's body is propelled like that of a pole vaulter's into suspension when that occurs. Whatever suspension does take place follows the straightening of this leg but it is not a usual part of the sustained gallop.

Despite the fact that the non-diagonal back pad strikes

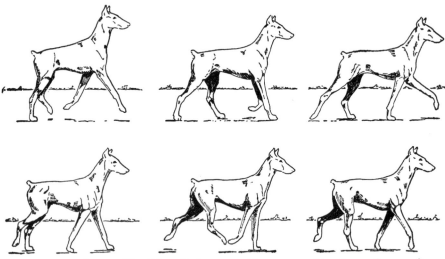

THE CANTER—The Doberman illustrates this three-time gait. First he takes off with three feet leaving the right rear as the sole support. In the second position the right diagonal has come into play and stands alone in the third position. The fourth brings the left front down and in the fifth this carries the entire weight. In the sixth, we have a partial but not a full left diagonal. The sequence may be reversed in order with the front leg that is detached from the diagonal being the "leading leg."

the ground first after suspension, it is the non-leading leg that absorbs the concussion of momentum and is susceptible to sprains of the suspensory and inferior carpal ligaments. Should the leading leg become sprained it is usually due to over-reach or rough ground.

A dog turns into his leading leg, otherwise he is apt to trip. Afield, he will collect and shift his lead if he has time rather than turn away from it and toward the non-leading leg. Many riders throw their horses by forcing them to turn on a "false lead" but the dog usually has more sense than a green rider.

When making a turn at high speed, the dog's body is catapulted over the leading leg which transcribes what is equivalent to an arc in relation to the shoulder which actually moves, and the transcribing point or pad remains fixed. As the radius line of the leg reaches or enters the back half of the sector thus formed, the weight of the body is pivoted on this support by shift of weight, cross reach of the non-leading front leg, turn of head and neck, and is then completed by the push from the back leg opposite the leading front leg.

Though that is modified as to exact position of legs by quick or slow turns, the foundation action remains the same for all turns on the forehand. Dogs rarely make a turn on the rearhand as will horses under training and handled by a good rider who lifts the weight off the forehand and more or less spins the horse in the direction of the leading front leg. This is often seen on the polo field and may at times be used by dogs when emergency demands.

THE NORMAL GALLOP

The sustained gallop or canter moves almost imperceptibly into the normal gallop, the difference being merely the splitting of the diagonal so that the gait becomes four-time. There are four distinct phases of body support in the normal gallop, which is also identical with that of the horse, and these at times receive or render slight aid one to the other.

The supports are *left rear, right rear, left front* and

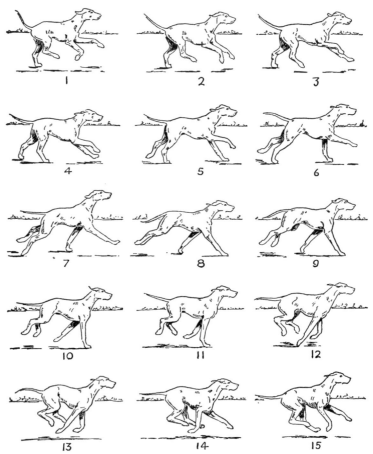

THE GALLOP—The Pointer illustrates this four-time gait. In positions 1, 2 and 3 the support is the left rear; in 4 it is left and right rear; in 5 and 6 it is left diagonal; in 7 it is left front; in 8 and 9 it is left and right front; in 10 and 11 it is right front; 12 shows the take-off for suspension and 13, 14 and 15 show suspension. Each position is contemplated to consume equal time and this dog is leading with the right front leg.

right front; the latter is the leading leg in this sequence. The order will be changed by the shift of the leading leg. Had this been a sustained gallop, the diagonal under the first listed sequence would have been the right rear and left front but the latter is now acting enough in advance of the rear to change the timing.

Suspension takes place just after the straightening of the leading leg. Its degree is due to two forces: one created by the leverage action in the actual straightening of the leg in which push comes as much from the long phalanges or "hare-foot" as the shoulder; the other is momentum created by the one-two push given by the back legs catapulting the body over the non-leading front leg onto the leading leg. The stride of the normal gallop is apt to be twice that of the sustained in any given dog due to suspension and the increased reach of each leg which momentum necessitates.

It can be noted from this sequence that in neither the sustained or normal gallop will both the front and rear legs be extended at the same time as many of the old artists depicted their dogs and horses. All four legs will, at one stage, be collected or drawn up under the dog. There is a time, however, when both front legs are forward and both back legs extended backward but the two positions never coincide with one another. In each, the legs are in the process of passing, one moving forward and the other backward.

The Thoroughbred horse is the greatest exponent of the normal style gallop among domestic animals. A study of his conformation as seen on the race tracks and around hunt clubs should be revealing. The conformation found on the seven furlong sprinter, though within the same general range, is different from that on the horse going a mile and sixteenth or better. Occasionally one sees a horse capable of running both short and long races, but he is usually one that can cruise and lay-off the early pace to finish with a burst of speed down the stretch. There is a difference in all three and that same difference can give us ideas for our dogs.

The average dog breeder can learn more from the Thoroughbred hunter than the racer, for these with their ability to cover all types of ground at the most profitable and applicable speed and style can be more prognostic to the sporting, hound, working and terrier breeders. Certainly an eye for a good middle-weight hunter will never miss a tireless Beagle, Foxhound or bird dog.

While the leading front leg supports the body for one-third of the entire time required for the complete sequence and the non-leading front is usually the first to be injured, the power of the gallop is derived from the straightening of the back legs, the one opposite the leading leg supporting the body for the next longest period. These back legs not only impart the drive to suspension but one of them contacts the ground and takes over the shock and support at its end.

The power in the back legs comes from two factors: extended length of leg over contracted position which is governed by angulation, and a set of muscles known as the "rearing muscles" which are those used by a dog when he stands on his back legs with his front feet waving at you.

THE DOUBLE SUSPENSION GALLOP

The gazehounds and occasionally some of the other breeds, notably Dobermans, use the leaping style gallop. This is also a four-time gait with four distinct supports for the body weight. However, it differs in several respects from the two other forms.

The supports are *right rear, left rear, left front* and then *right front*. In this, you will note a variation in the order of support; the first front support comes on the same side as the last rear support and not the opposite. While the order of the normal gallop will appear in the leaping style, the results are never as good, for the leading front leg cannot be alternated as readily with each complete sequence which lessens the strain.

The major difference between this gait and others is that it has two distinct periods of suspension during each sequence. One follows the straightening of the leading foreleg and the other the straightening of the opposite back leg. This gives the pronounced increase in speed over the normal style gallop. In this you will see all four legs extended at the same time as well as contracted; one leg has completed its travel in the given direction and started back to pass the other just arriving.

The leaping style gallop has certain physical requirements not demanded by the normal gallop. The dog must be able to get his back feet well under him without the disadvantages of a steep croup, particularly for early speed, so we find the Whippet with an arched but not roached back line. Distance runners in this style though will have a flatter back line as will be noted in the Greyhounds on the tracks and used in coursing jack-rabbits. These dogs also have considerable tuck-up but this is more apparent than true due to the deep brisket.

The *rearing muscles,* those which straighten the back legs and the entire back line, are specifically important to this gait and must be as powerful as is possible to get on the given dog. When the right or left back pad takes over the job of supporting the dog's body, the weight of the whole body is carried by these muscles and they must relift the fore part of the body back above the horizontal level.

Both the front and rear legs must have greater freedom of action, their forward reach and follow-through being more pronounced in this than other styles; the pad transcribes a long arc.

There is no doubt about this being the fastest style of

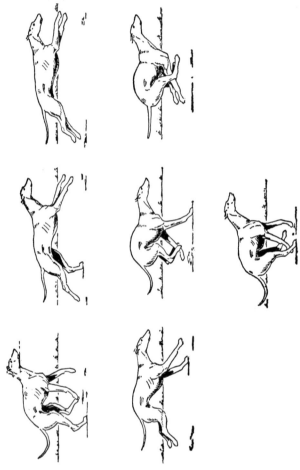

THE DOUBLE SUSPENSION GALLOP—The Greyhound is shown in the positions of this four-time, double suspension gait. The first position shows the right rear support, the second shows the left rear. Suspension follows this and the dog lands on the left front and then transfers his weight to the right front from which he takes off for another period of suspension coming down on the right rear. This sequence may vary slightly with individuals. Note that it is the only gait in which all four legs appear extended or fully contracted.

gallop but it is also the most fatiguing. Apparently there has been very little change over the centuries in the general conformation of the breeds using this style from which we might conclude that we have come to the best answer. That, however, is not the case for there is more room for improvement in this than any other style now being used. Either in early speed, endurance or a combination of both, the animals of the wild that use this style are far superior, pound for pound, to the Whippet, Greyhound, Saluki, and others using it.

The cheetah gives us one of our best comparisons. A leopard-like animal found in Persia, India and Africa, it is approximately the same size as our larger gazehounds and differs from the cat family in that its feet are like those of a dog. The natives train it for use in capturing antelope and other game. A good cheetah is at least 5 per cent faster than our best Greyhounds.

The three-prong antelope is the fastest and most proficient user of this style. His conformation not only makes for top speed but also for endurance. This fellow has been clocked at 60 miles per hour and he can cruise at forty-five. In a mile race, he would be under the wire before Man O'War, Seabiscuit, Whirlaway or Assault had rounded into the stretch which might be called "winning going away."

The mountain lion which roves the Rockies uses this style; he has exceptionally early speed but cannot last for any distance. His initial sequences measure upwards of 30 feet or slightly better than a horse's.

The jack-rabbit, no mean performer at this style, is likely the fastest, pound for pound. He can flash away at 45 miles per hour, five or ten above a coyote's top speed but he usually winds up in the coyote's stomach. The race is not always to the swift and the jack tires comparatively quickly. Perhaps that is due to the long hock assembly which does put zip in his first few leaps but takes a lot out of him.

COMPARATIVE SPEEDS

These wild animals have been clocked by automobile or over distances that could be measured approximately while being watched through glasses. The speeds which naturalists give us for them may not be as accurate as the stop-watch times of our race tracks. However, one is running over rough terrain or down creek beds while the other is on a prepared track. Yet a comparison of their times reduced to one mile may be enlightening. They are: Thoroughbred hunter over the 4½-mile Maryland Hunt Cup's course, 2:27; trotting horse, 1:58; pacing horse, 1:55; coyote over distance, 1:50; running horse, 1:35; white-tailed deer, 1:33; coyote sprinting, 1:30; pronghorn cruising, 1:30; jack-rabbit sprinting, 1:20; cheetah at top speed, 1:32; pronghorn at top speed, 1:00.

There is verification of a moose putting five miles of riverbed under him in 12 minutes without breaking from a trot and not being prodded beyond the first flush. That is a rate of 2:24 per mile.

The wild animals which had been clocked were not selected as the swiftest of their type but the clocker took whatever he came in contact with afield. That is not the case with the times of horses and dogs, for these were made in competitive racing. This indicates that wild animals have a more perfect pattern of construction in general—they probably needed this to survive the problems of their existence.

Compared with these times, we can use those of the Greyhound and Whippet, probably the fastest of our gazehounds. The Greyhound runs the quarter-mile in approximately 25 seconds depending on the track, which if maintained for a mile rates 1:40 but they cannot hold that speed. The Greyhound futurity is 495 yards as compared to the 440 quarter, and the time goes up to 28 seconds which is at the rate of 1:44; so you can see how an additional 51 yards cuts the time. The Whippet's best short times prolonged check around 1:43.

We have had no comparative tests, but for sheer speed and endurance the night running hounds of the mountains and Southern and Midwestern sections would likely take the honors. They will keep a prey moving for 24 to 36 hours. Their initial speed does not equal a horse's, but they would get our money over a five or six-mile natural course. Some of the Foxhounds in hunt packs at clubs may be just as good but a pack hound lacks the individuality of a lone runner, otherwise he would not be a pack hound.

There is an amusing angle to this: If one of these good-going Walkers, Red Bones or Blue Ticks was brought into a show ring, both judge and ringsiders would exclaim: "Where did that mutt come from!" The same might be said of the Pointers and Setters which top the big field trial stakes from Canada to the Mexican Border —these dogs can work the brush, covering from 35 to 45 miles in three hours, finding and handling birds along the way. Any good field trial bird dog should be able to work his ground at upwards of 20 miles per hour for two to three hours.

From time to time in this study we will emphasize the factors of speed, for speed means effective locomotion. We have no more practical means of judging it regardless of the problem or breed involved—Scottie or Dachs going to ground, Pointer or spaniel afield. Likewise its factors are also the factors of agility and effective movement. That applies to Chihuahua and Dane alike.

6

Locomotion

MOVEMENT is far more than picking them up and putting them down; it is a successive change of position employing all laws of motion. The dog's gaits—the act or power of moving from place to place whether across the rug or the field—are specifically locomotion. Locomotion, however, is purely a process of falling, but falling in the right direction ,stopping at the right time and landing in the right place, that is, controlled falling.

The study of locomotion brings us face to face with two factors: speed and power, which are at the two extremes of the subject. We cannot think of them as single factors but must consider both as a blend, either on the bitter or the sweet side, whichever way you like your " 'alf 'nd 'alf."

"Speed? Do you think I'm running my Scotties in the Whippet races?" one may challenge.

"Humn—I'm not hitching my Poms to a milk cart."

The majority may think of speed in terms of the race track, and of power in those of the draft animal . . . the flash of a nose between the electric eyes of a finish line . . . plodding horses dragging broad-wheeled carts through the aroma of new-mown hay. Actually the pattern of these principles as applied to locomotion can be split at some point near a theoretic center, one side designated as *speed* and the other as *power*. As we use these terms in discussing locomotion and gaits, we will be indicating the tendency toward one of these two factors rather than the extreme of either. To give grace to the powerful animal, we must secure the elements of speed, while to increase endurance requires some of the factors of power.

It has been established that the timing of locomotion, that is leg action, is the same in all dogs with exception of the gazehounds, also that the mechanical action and principles are the same as used by other four-legged animals. So we can make many direct comparisons with these animals, in whole and in part.

THE CENTER OF GRAVITY

We will also refer quite often to the *center of gravity;* it plays a most important part. This is an imaginary point about which all forces are equal, united about a focus. In the dog's body it is a point on which, if the body could be suspended, the entire structure would remain in perfect balance. It is also that point in the front or rear assembly in which the structure is in static or stationary balance and all opposing forces are equal. The latter we will consider when we start to break down the component parts of the body, but at this time when we speak of the *center of gravity* we will mean that of the entire body.

The exact location of this center is not very important so long as we understand the changes that any variation of it will make. Its approximate location in the majority of dogs in stationary position is in the center of the body at a point where a vertical line just back of the shoulder assembly intersects a line dividing the upper two-thirds of the body from the lower third. This will vary with the length and weight of head and neck, the length of legs and the general structure of the torso. Momentum will also change it when the dog is in motion, moving it forward.

We can never quite appreciate the elements of locomotion unless we are conscious of this center and understand the effects any change in it produces. Therefore, we cannot emphasize its importance too much. Swing a 50-

pound bag of dog food to your right shoulder—that changes the center of gravity of your body—and it is much easier to walk if your body is twisted slightly to the left than if you continue in the natural vertical posture.

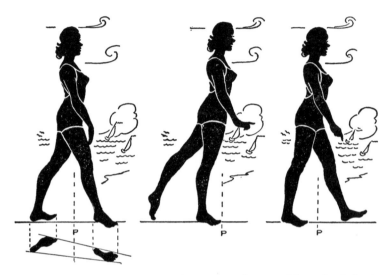

WALKING IS FALLING—In the first position the lady is standing on the full base of support with the center of gravity perpendicular (P) directly under her body. Next she straightens the left leg forcing the center of gravity up and forward while the right leg acts somewhat like the spoke in a wheel. The center of gravity travels in an arc and eventually starts downward and beyond the front base of support. To arrest this the left leg continues forward and takes over its share of body support. In the last half of the described arc, the center of gravity is falling.

Now, for this walking-falling idea, perhaps we can illustrate by asking a lady to take a step. She stands with feet separated as though she came to rest after the last step. Her body weight is distributed over the base support established by the area between the forward foot and the one to the rear. If each leg bears equal weight, a perpendicular line from the center of this area passes through the center of gravity of her body. She straightens the leg directed toward the rear and, by this action, pushes the center of gravity upward and forward over an arc which is prescribed by the other leg as it acts as a spoke in a wheel might do.

When the center reaches a point in this arc slightly beyond the vertical radius of the forward leg, it then begins to fall along the line of the arc. Unless it is arrested, the lady will land on her face for the last part of this travel is definitely falling. She swings forward the leg that started it all and puts a stop to it in time for the other leg to forget being a radius and get into action.

Keep in mind that the center of gravity has transcribed an arc from the low point in the starting position upward and then downward to the same level at completion of the stride. This must be lifted, dropped and then relifted. The nearer this arc resembles a flat plane and retains the same given travel, the less muscular effort will be required. That is a very important factor to remember when considering a dog's gait.

The same mechanical actions take place when the dog moves. The front legs are called upon to do most of the relifting and absorbing of the force of gravity and momentum. That is why the front experiences more injuries than the rear. Dogs and horses both break down in front long before the rear goes.

Referring back to the sequence of the fast gaits, you will note that one of the dog's back legs takes the first shock of the momentum in the natural gallop and one of the two shocks in the leaping style gallop, but in each case as the center of gravity is raised the dog is catapulted over a front leg as though it were a pole used by a vaulter. Much of the relifting is done by the back legs, even in the slower gaits, by the action of the rearing muscles.

The thrust imparted by the back leg is dependent on the leg's length when fully extended compared to that when contracted to the minimum in the stride. This means acute angulation, particularly of the upper and lower thigh sections. It also might suggest angulation at the hock joint, but horsemen have long countered the latter with a demand for "straight dropped hocks" because they assure us that the joint can be straightened which is of utmost importance.

THE LAW OF GRAVITY

The center of gravity always descends at the same rate of speed, for this is the *law of gravity* coming into play. If you arrange to drop a bullet from the muzzle of a gun at the exact instant one is shot from it, without trajectory or a rising arc, both bullets will strike the ground at the same instant, though one will be quite in advance of the other. Momentum or suspension gives us this increased distance.

We get greater distance for the bullet by an arc of trajectory but too much arc will produce a lob and shorten the distance from start to finish. We have and will stress this fact numerous times in discussing gaits for it has a decided bearing on their efficiency.

There is an old barroom teaser that often wins bets as well as illustrates this fact about gravity. To prove how steady your hand is, you can flip two beer caps from the edge of the table, making one hit beyond a mark some two or three yards away and the other less than half the distance, yet both to hit the floor on the same instant. You shoot one with your right hand and one with the left hand. The secret is to hit both of the caps at the same time though you hit one much harder. It may take a try or two to get both fingers flipping at the same time with more pressure being put on one than on the other, but you can at least become proficient enough to convince yourself that this is an inflexible law. Keep this factor in mind as you analyze gaits and locomotion.

The dog has only three means of combatting the pull of gravity. One is by sending the center of gravity over a high arc as is done with the rifle bullet when we raise our rear sights and shoot at a slight upward angle. The distance we get from a given charge in a shell is governed by the arc or trajectory thus formed.

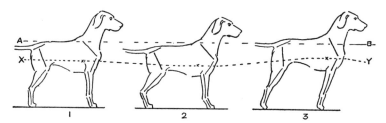

RISE AND FALL OF CENTER OF GRAVITY—The Pointer shows the normal center of gravity level in position 1 this being indicated by the small "X" back of the shoulders. Position 2 shows this CG at its lowest when either a diagonal or lateral support is directly under their body terminals, for the legs are contracted at this point. They straighten as in position 3 and lift the CG to its highest point. Line A-B shows the rise and fall of the withers by comparison which indicates the arc described by the CG.

A certain amount of lift is necessary, but like raising the trajectory of the rifle bullet so that it covers only half its normal yardage, too much lift will reduce the dog's efficiency in both casual and working gaits. We see this all too often in local dogs which come out for the shooting stakes at field trials. Straight-shouldered animals, these fellows, that lob across the field like bouncing balls. Though they can get lift from the "rearing muscles" of the loins and back legs, the straight shoulders are likely the dominating contribution to the fault, which certainly produces too much fatigue.

The second method used by a dog to overcome the pull of gravity is sheer momentum which provides distance with a flatter arc. This comes specifically from his rearing muscles but the animal must have the proper shoulder structure in order to employ this power along the line of progress.

RISE AND FALL OF THE WITHERS

The crotch of a rail fence has long been an ideal place to sit and let the rest of the world go by, or to watch dogs working afield.

"Dat white 'n' liver pup ain't never gonna be no good," old Henry, a Negro sage, once informed this writer from his perch on the next crotch as we watched two young derbies follow an older dog through the sedge of a field below us.

"What makes you think so? He comes from two of the best field trial Pointers that we've ever cut loose."

"Mebbe he do, but look at dem withers a bobbing up 'n' down lak Miss Irene's rocking chair. He ain't wuth his training."

Henry proved to be right; the pup was a washout for endurance. The reason was that he expended most of his energy in lifting his center of gravity rather than pro- pelling it along the line of travel. His arc was not flat enough for effective travel. He fought a battle against gravity without progress. There are several structural factors, particularly in the forequarters, which bring about this result. Fatigue will cause a marked rise and fall of an animal's withers no matter how good might be its angu- lation and conformation.

"Keep your eye on a horse's withers," a racing trainer once told us, "and you can tell exactly when he begins to peter out. No rocking horse ever won a stake race . . . he's got to keep running level to bring home the bacon."

If you will take notice of this the next time you are at the race track, you will find this statement pretty accu- rate. Particularly in the longer races, you can spot the horses that have made their bids but do not have what it takes to be up there at the finish. Watch the stragglers which have set an early pace and then faded as they come bobbing home a little late for dinner.

We once saw a well known Setter cut loose at a field trial streak out across the open and into the cover, working it to the far edges, then swing back into the bird-field

THE ROCKING HORSE—Both the Setter and Pointer shown in this sketch are making an excessive effort to lift their center of gravity. The Setter is doing it with the front assembly while the Pointer is using his rearing muscles and the back assembly. Either one will resemble a rocking horse going across the field and both lack endurance going up rather than out along the line of progress.

with more time than usual for combing that. All along he had seemed to be gliding rather than galloping.

The very next brace brought out a dog which at a casual glance might have been his twin, but the moment he was cut loose the resemblance ceased, for even in the open he ran is if leaping a fence at each stride. He scarcely penetrated the cover, never reached the edges, cut the course and flopped into the bird-field just as the time limit expired. He had worked much harder every minute of the time but got nowhere except up and down, wearing himself out doing it.

The major cause of the excess rise and fall of the withers is improper conformation and angulation, especially the conforming of the front and rear assemblies to one another. Two factors, thrust and lift, are involved, and they must be synchronized for efficiency. Fatigue will eventually disrupt this balance in any animal and induce a pronounced rise and fall.

The third method by which a dog combats gravity is by continuous support; that is, at all times there is vertical support for both the front and back part of its body. When the dog is walking, you can scarcely notice a rise and fall because the body is always supported by three legs. In the trot and pace, it will have the front and back support except where suspension occurs. When suspension does occur, the rise and fall is apt to be more pronounced even when the dog is moving correctly. The arc of the trajectory is carried higher so that the dog's body is carried a greater distance before it is necessary for the legs to take over the support.

We cannot prevent a certain rise and fall in any gait, particularly in fast ones. Too much of it, though, either indicates or produces fatigue and the conformation that contributes to it should be avoided. In addition to the fact that the dog resorts to it when his front legs will not stand the concussion of the momentum in the flat arc, the location of the *center of gravity* affects it.

The juggling of this center is only slightly changed to produce any given or desired results. A number of things will change its location. Moving it forward increases speed—this is done by high withers, a long neck, long head or anything that brings weight forward. Endurance may be heightened by moving it backward and putting weight on the rearhand. Of course, any of these changes must be within the boundary of efficient conformation.

INSTABILITY CREATES POWER AND SPEED

This change affects equilibrium and, strange as it may seem, both speed and pulling power are intensified by instability of equilibrium rather than by stability. Endurance is somewhat enhanced by a degree of stability. Primarily in all dogs you seek instability and not stability of equilibrium, but this must be of such nature as can be directed along the line of locomotion.

Let me cite one type of carnival side-show, which will serve to teach a lesson about instability and the principles of locomotion. Always billed as "The World's Tug-of-war Champion," a medium sized, broad shouldered chap would strut into the sawdust arena, arrogant and insulting as he paraded about in a leopard skin and sandled feet, adjusting silver arm bands.

"See this little man," the barker heckled, "all strength, all muscle—this Zito, the powerful, he will defeat any man in this town at the tug-of-war. Bring on the biggest, strongest man you have—ah, this big fellow right here, he is so strong but Zito will drag him out of the ring as he would a child."

Here the barker frowns and acts sympathetic before he finally exclaims: "To make things equal, we will handicap this Zito. We will make him carry another man on his back, then see if this big fellow can't defeat him!"

In time all the dimes were collected and the spiel came to an end. Perhaps it was the village blacksmith who squared off with this cocky bantam in the battle of the century. The little man would take the barker, a rather huge chap, on his shoulders and for a few minutes it was nip and tuck as they gave the audience a little play for their money. One or twice it would seem that the blacksmith might win but there came a time when the barker leaned forward and the bantam walked right out of the arena dragging the blacksmith as though he were a child.

INSTABILITY—It is not the little man's strength that enables him to pull the big fellow at will but the leverage action applied by the instability created when the man on his shoulders leans forward. This creates an instability of equilibrium resulting in a force too great for the other to overcome.

It was not Zito's strength but the weight of the barker on his shoulders which created an instability of equilibrium resulting in a force too great for the blacksmith to overcome.

A horse will move a heavier load when a firm, rather tight rein is held than when he is given a free head because this puts weight on the forehand and results in greater instability. The old teamster often got down off his wagon seat in a hard pull, climbed upon the end of the tongue so that he could throw his weight onto the horses' necks and bring about the same results.

The American jockey uses a crouched seat with his weight carried forward to put weight on the forehand and increase speed by instability. The more upright seat of the "hill and dale" rider is used to produce greater stability and lessen fatigue for he seeks a compromise between the two factors even as many dog breeders must.

Skaters give us another illustration of this factor—the sprinter leans as far forward as he possibly can while the distance man does not, in the effort to blend speed with endurance.

In these, we have two major factors to keep in the back of our minds as we delve into the mechanics involved in the movements of our dogs: the arc created by the travel of the *center of gravity* and the comparative weight of the forepart of the body with that of the rear.

British and French equestrian experts who have made a study of horses in regard to distribution of weight have concluded that the ratio ranges from five pounds on the forehand for every four pounds on the rearhand up to four to three. This will hold true in the majority of dogs. In the gazehounds, though, this will go as high as three to two, the speed being increased as the ratio mounts.

We do not have jockeys and teamsters to shift this center of gravity in our dogs in order to vary the degree of instability desired. It is solely by conformation that we can effect this result.

Instability or weight on the forehand is increased by low withers, long legs, light body, high croup, long neck and head, low carriage of neck and head, deep brisket, and momentum. These all move the center of gravity forward and increase speed at the expense of endurance.

Stability or "weight off the forehand," moving the center of gravity backward, is obtained by the inverse of these. As this increases endurance, it is desirable to a varied degree in all dogs. The purpose of the dog marks the features and degrees of each that are to be stressed. As a rule high withers and deep briskets get a call, for the former increases shoulder-blade space and the latter gives more heart room, two valuable assets.

THE LAWS OF LEVERAGE

Movement itself is accomplished by the leverage action of the bones which are propelled by the muscles. The dog is literally jacked along by these as one might a box with a crowbar. In the action we encounter the three basic *laws of leverage* for they are present in the slightest movement of any part of the dog's body. These three laws are too important not to receive full consideration.

The first of these orders is known as *PFW* in which the fulcrum comes between the power being applied and the weight to be lifted or moved. The seesaw is a specific illustration. Even though you do remember these laws from physics, it will not be time wasted to refresh our minds on their general application.

Place a short stick over some sharp edged support to study the first order. On one end of the stick hang a weight and apply the power by hand to the other end. When you move the weight *(W)* away from the fulcrum *(F)*, you will note that it takes more power *(P)* to sustain or raise it, but it is also evident that the same power or movement of P over the same distance produces greater action in W.

The second order is PWF in which the weight comes between the fulcrum and power as it does in a wheelbarrow. Place the point of the stick on the sharp-edged

THE THREE ORDERS OF LEVERAGE—PFW, PWF and WPF. If you make simple tests of these orders, you will find that the closer you bring P to F the more action you will give to W by equal movements of P but greater power is required to make the move. A saving of power would be called a mechanical advantage. But nature always chooses to apply it to a mechanical disadvantage, so if we seek endurance in the dog we have to change this slightly which is done by short hocks and other features requested.

fulcrum, holding the other end in your hand. Hang the weight at various locations on it and observe that it seems lighter when closest to F and heaviest when nearest to P. In this, as in the first order, the same movement of P produces more action on W when it is farthest from F but this produces fatigue more quickly than when W is close to F.

The third order is WPF. Place one end of the stick on the fulcrum, grasp it a short way out and hang the weight on the other end. By the same manipulation of W, we will arrive at the same conclusions as in the first two orders as to the ratios between WF and FP.

It is an unchangeable law of all levers that the shorter WF is in comparison to PF, the less is the power required but also the distance of travel from a given action is reduced. Therefore a short WF and long PF work to a mechanical advantage, a long WF and a short PF to a mechanical disadvantage and hasten fatigue in the dog.

All applications of levers in nature, our dogs included, work to a mechanical disadvantage because it is more important to get speed and action than to preserve energy.

In the breakdown analysis of the front and rear assemblies, we shall consider these laws in their specific application, but for the present we will concern ourselves only with the fact that they work for action at the cost of fatigue. Power and maximum endurance give way to action and speed and more particularly to convenience of form.

MECHANICAL DISAD- VANTAGE—By tripling the length of the os calcis in the back leg we can make it work to a mechanical advantage, but the muscle would not have action enough to move it the same distance as before. Nature is not concerned with the peculiar appearance of this back leg but she does want action and gets it at a mechanical disadvantage in the hock that we normally see.

We can appreciate the latter by a glance at the action of the dog's hock joint. This joint is activated by a muscle which originates on the upper thigh, passes along the lower thigh and applies its power to the tip of the hock or *os calcis*. In the stride, the contact of the pad with the ground is F, where the lower thigh contacts the hock is W and the tip of the *os calcis* is P.

If we triple the length of the *os calcis* the leverage action would work to an advantage but the muscular action would not be sufficient to straighten the hock joint and the movement of the pad would be reduced to one-third its present amount. It is because of action and not because nature thought the extended *os calcis* looked like a monstrosity, that mechanical advantage was sacrificed for speed.

You will find this same sacrifice present in every bone and muscle placement in the dog. Therefore, we cannot but conclude that nature intended the animal, whether a Toy Manchester or a Bull Mastiff, for action and that the factors of speed are the dominating ones in all dogs.

THE DRAFT DOG

As a draft animal the dog presents a different problem in locomotion from the one used as a pet or a hunter. Maybe nature never intended dogs for draft—she never contemplated that we would wear glasses yet she put our ears in the right place for them. So it must have been with dogs, for they have done a pretty good job over the years turning spits, pulling milk carts and streaking across the Arctic with heavily loaded sledges.

Actually the dog pushes rather than pulls the load despite dictionary definitions. The power originates where the back foot is in contact with the ground; its force is from that point to the collar hitch in the form of a push. However, it is transmitted through the bones of the leg and back to the shoulder assembly.

There is less loss of force if transmitted over a straight line and, if this cannot be done, through a series of angles as small as can be set up. This indicates a croup with upward of 40-degree slope with rather straight stifles and hock.

Standards for draft breeds usually ask for stifles "well let down," which is asking for a long thigh with its accompanying longer muscles. Stifles well let down will often result in less angulation at this joint and also at the hocks. Another means of improving the length of activating muscles on the thigh will be a longer pelvis frame with the points well aft of the thigh joint.

We once saw a husky taken into the group at a dog show when the judge chided the handler for bringing such a horrible specimen in the class. Perhaps he was rather terrible, being straight of stifle and hock, but he had been one of Father Hubbard's lead dogs in Alaska and we had seen him without help move a sledge with ten bags of dog food on it. His physical conformation was far from that of a shepherd but rather resembled that of a Percheron horse. This conformation, which will vary for the dogs used for fast driving in draft, should then lean more to that of the Standardbred trotter, going back to the 30-degree croup with more angulation in the stifle.

Until one has experienced it he can hardly appreciate the pleasure of a dog team hooked to a sledge. Think of trees hanging heavy with snow, fences top-wire deep in drifts, mountain sides tumbling drunkenly, distant horizons grey-blended into sky, while down a broken trail line, in and out among the pines, their breath bouquets on the sharp air, race ten white and biscuit Eskimos with traces taut and red plumes a warm contrast against the cold. At the moment you cling to the Peterborough sledge in this wild precipitous dash, you will not worry much about the bend of stifle or hock.

7

Lateral Displacement

THE passenger on the big airliner lowered his magazine and gazed out the window at the approaching city coming steadily toward him as though it might climb into his lap. Perhaps he never questioned why this plane with its two powerful motors drawing it straight ahead was sidling up to its destination as a horse might to a dismounting block. There was a counterforce being applied to it by cross-winds of which the pilot was thoroughly conscious though they were given little or no consideration by the passengers.

These cross-winds had to be counteracted by a change in the direction of the plane's thrust, angling to the right or left to offset the drift in the opposite direction. There is a transverse force, similar to the cross-winds, present at all times in every gait the dog employs. Like the rise and fall of the withers, this force cannot be completely eliminated; it can only be recognized for what it is and its effect on the dog appreciated.

The force, *lateral displacement,* is as important in a dog's gait as any other faculty. It has its effect on speed, leg action, pulling ability and endurance. The character of a dog's movement to and from you is particularly influenced by it. Yet this has been given less consideration by dog breeders than any agent present in movement.

When the dog stands motionless, the four leg supports create a rectangular base. If the weight was equally distributed over this base, the center of gravity would fall on the intersection of the diagonal bisectors. It is not evenly distributed, and the center is forward of this intersection a distance governed by the factors which put weight on or take it off the forehand. However, the pivotal point of the body or base support is at this intersection and the center of gravity acts as an overhang to it.

This condition might not produce lateral displacement if all four legs acted so that the power transmitted from

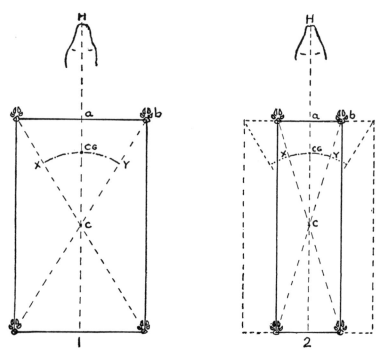

LATERAL DISPLACEMENT—Sketch 1. The rectangle represents the base of support. The Center of Gravity, being forward of the intersection of the diagonals will, in motion, swing from right to left over the arc XY from diagonal to diagonal. Sketch 2. This action is shortened when the rectangle is made narrower in the case where the feet come closer to the center line of support in travel. The nearer the feet fall to this line, the shorter will be the arc XY. Lengthening AH will move CG forward and lengthen XY, creating instability and speed but increasing the force of lateral displacement. The mechanical effect of single tracking can be measured in the triangle abc by the comparative length of ab.

them was equalized at all times and directed along the line of locomotion. Only in the pace is this approximated, which probably accounts for the fact that dogs take to the pace when tired and out of condition.

Because of leg action, power application, and the position of the center of gravity, the latter swings from right to left in an arc with a radius pivoting on the center of the rectangle and bound by the location of the two diagonals. The movement of the center of gravity along this arc is *lateral displacement*.

You can make a practical test of its effect by picking up a 25-pound bag of dog food, holding it in front of your body and running across the lawn. You will find that the bag tends to swing to right and left and throw you off balance. Its hindrance is increased by extending the bag farther out from your body. It is minimized by holding the bag close to the body and by trying to get the feet placed under it and as nearly in its lateral center as possible. You will not be wasting time in making a few experimental sprints with the bag, for they will heighten appreciation for some of the things that we shall point out about this force.

This force accounts for the characteristic "roll" of some breeds and the animal is more or less letting it have its way without utilizing too much muscular effort to check it. In a few cases, this may be the best answer for the dog if it is not too pronounced. We have seen field trial bird dogs cast away showing no indication of it at the time; then they seem to be twisting in two parts as they plod back from the bird field and course. On the same course others, manifesting it to a degree from the very start, often finished in better condition for they had not burnt themselves out fighting it, although they could not have been considered good ground coverers.

That little snakey twist you might see to the back line as you look down on a dog going away is due to this force.

The animal which fights it with muscular effort may stand true in front when not in motion but move decidedly "out at the elbows" in an effort to counteract it.

COMBATTING DISPLACEMENT

Dogs and other quadrupeds combat this force in a number of different ways, some of which are accomplished by conformation and others by muscular and leg action or a combination of both.

First we might consider the things that increase it. One, quite important to speed, is that when the center of gravity is moved forward the arc is carried toward the base or widest part of the inscribed triangle; and this is one time that you want the least part of it. Quite logically a wide base of support or rectangle lengthens the arc and increases the force.

A few draft animals with a wide base of support may sometimes be seen to utilize it to advantage in a heavy pull by rolling the shoulders with it and letting it add to the force being generated by the opposite back leg. While this may be an occasional asset to the draft, its advantage to dogs is so minute that it can be dismissed.

We have seen the advantage to other factors of the gaits in having a forward center of gravity to create instability, therefore, for efficiency of the gaits, we are more interested in other means of reducing lateral displacement while retaining this feature which increases it. Thus we have the advantage of one with a compensating factor.

Mathematically—and nature takes advantage of this in all of her fast children—the most logical means of reducing it is to narrow the rectangle physically or actively and in turn shorten the arc. That means, more than any other, is the one employed by efficient movers.

We once criticized a horse for being too narrow in front and were quickly put in our place by an old timer with the remark, "A horse can't be too narrow in front so long as he has lung room and moves true."

This old timer's remark is substantiated by the structure found on such effective speed merchants as the cheetah, Greyhound, pronghorn antelope, Thoroughbred horse and others. We have found many dog breeders and a few horsemen who frowned on this feature without analyzing its value. Heart and lung room must be present, but this can be had in the vast majority of breeds without resorting to width, means of which will be discussed in the specific break-down of the body.

The Bulldog, the Scottie and other low-set dogs cannot be selected with the idea of narrowing the physical rectangle, but this force can be utilized by them in the final kill of their prey in the same manner that the draft horse uses it in pulling, that is, by letting it swing and add to the shaking motion. The majority of breeds, however, can have a narrow front without sacrifice of general characteristics of the type or any loss to heart and lung room. Thus they reduce the undesirable effects of this force.

As revealed by the study of gaits, the dog has three general types of body support by the legs.

The first finds him standing still, supported by all four legs with the pads planted at the corners of a quadrangle. This can be likened to the support of a table and as we progress with this study, keep in mind the unstable stance of a table from which one leg has been removed. The support by all four legs does not appear at any time when the dog is moving; he always lacks one or more of these supports.

In the walk and canter, the dog will often have three feet on the ground. They may not be placed solidly but one is just leaving the ground or contacting it while two others support the body. This gives him a three-point support which might be likened to the tripod or tricycle. Its efficiency however is not as positive as the tripod because the legs in natural progress cannot be readjusted to compensate for the ground. Were it not continuous movement, the dog in these positions would be as wabbly as a three-legged table.

At other times in all gaits from the slow walk to the fast gallop, the body is supported either by two legs or by one leg. For instance, the right and left diagonals, the leading leg or the opposite back leg carry the weight. As the opposite back leg takes over after the leading leg, the two can be considered as a split diagonal support. The bicycle is the best illustration of this condition, but there is one important mechanical difference—the support of the bicycle runs in line, that of the dog shifts from right to left.

As this general class of support is used more often by the dog, especially in the fast gaits, its problems are a major factor in this study. We know that the bicycle would not give a smooth ride if the front or back wheel kept jumping to the right and left of the line of travel, so we can expect no more from the support of the dog's body when it is shifted from the right to left diagonal unless there is some compensating factor.

There is such a compensation. Nature gave it to us without equivocation. The dog does not shift the support from right to left as would be the case if his feet came down on the four corners of the base of support but he brings the pad marks as nearly in line with one another as is possible. This gives us a body support that is more nearly that of the bicycle and is spoken of usually as "single tracking."

This is an active means of combatting lateral displacement and giving the body a more secure support. At a slow walk or even trot this is not so evident but as speed mounts the pad marks will come nearer in line. It is a rare thing though that you find them positively in line but falling slightly to the left or right of the center line.

SINGLE TRACKING

Early one morning several years ago, we walked across
the track at Timonium with a trainer whose string of
two-year-olds was stabled there.   The hands were already
busy about the barns but only one set of hoof marks
showed on the freshly raked track.   As we came to these,

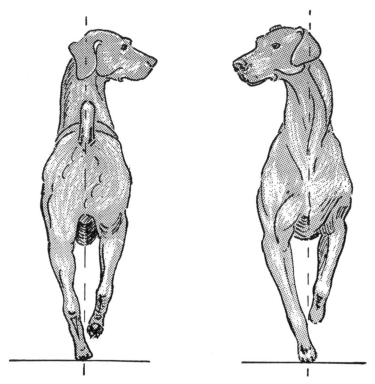

SINGLE TRACKING is illustrated by this German Short-
haired Pointer as he moves, coming and going.   Note that the
supporting foot is placed directly under the center of gravity
thus reducing the rectangle of the base of support to a minimum
width and likewise lateral displacement.   The legs should travel
in a true plane from shoulder and hip point to pad.   Also there
is no interference with the supporting ieg by the passing leg as
the latter is contracted.

old Slim suddenly let out a torrent of oaths, the veins on his temples popped out as if whiplashed as he pointed an accusing finger at the hoof marks.

"I told that damn boy to breeze the Graysteel colt and not to let him out—I'll fire him!"

"Hey!" we interrupted, puzzled as to the reasons for Slim forming his conclusions. "How the heck can you tell that the boy gave the colt its head?"

Slim's withering look made it evident that he could not understand how any man could be so ignorant. Then as he hurried off toward the barns, he gave a jumbled explanation that the hoof marks were too nearly in line for the colt to be breezing. You can walk around the track after a horse has been stabled and spot the very point where he had been given his head in the workout by this convergence on a single line.

The fox is one of the smoothest of movers whether at a trot or a gallop. Walk out across the fields after a light snow and pick up his tracks even when he was in a hurry. You can almost drop a chalk line touching both the right and left paw marks in the snow.

A young Standardbred trotter comes out for training and, as he stands near the starting point, you note his clean, straight legs, set almost vertically under his shoulder points. Two or three years pass and this colt has made a great name for himself. Watch him now as he is drawn to a halt in front of the judge's stand. Those legs are just as straight and just as clean but they are converging as they sweep down from body to ground so that he stands with front hoofs touching one another.

This "standing close," which has come on him gradually, was developed as the horse's speed mounted. The inward inclination does not start at the elbow but at the shoulder point; it has been caused by the animal's effort to get his support under the vertical center of gravity, off-setting lateral displacement and applying power directly on the line of locomotion.

MOVING CLOSE

What is true of horses and foxes in this respect is also true of dogs. Yet it is a fact not recognized or appreciated by the average breeder and exhibitor. Typical of these was a friend who not so long ago insisted that we must look at a sensational winner of the season.

"Watch his action," the friend beamed, "as he moves away from and toward you—it's marvelous! See how parallel his legs are, they are absolutely perpendicular to the ground."

The friend was right about the way the dog's legs moved and there was decidedly no effort on his part to get his pads and body support under his center of gravity. Perhaps, had the dog put his pads under that center for better body support, our friend would have said that he "moved too close." If we do not know the mechanical factors involved in this, our ideas are apt to be unsound.

At a leading Eastern show, an old time judge of working dogs not often seen in the German Shepherd ring, passed the red to the handler of an open class entrant, which was exceptionally well gaited, with the comment, "I liked him but he moved too close behind."

"But don't you know that Shepherds are supposed to single-track?" the handler protested.

The old judge patted him on the head with that look of tolerance one reserves for misinformed children one hasn't the time to set right, then turned to direct the steward for the next class.

It is not unusual in any field for ideas to become as fixed as sacred truths, passed on as traditions, without having a thorough analysis for soundness. This happens in business, manufacturing, engineering and sporting circles. In dogs, this idea about moving "too close" probably stems from such statements as is in the Fox Terrier Standard: *Both fore and hind legs should be carried straight forward in traveling, the stifles not turning outward.*

Animals moving at a slow walk or trot will not *single-track* but start the movement with the same vertical leg position as when standing still. As the speed increases, the legs gradually angle inward until the pads are finally falling on a line directly under the longitudinal center of the body. Some breeds or individuals may be more inclined than others to move the pad marks toward the single-track. A dog in good condition, all reflexes working, will develop this tendency as you apply field work to him. A seasoned campaigner, like the Standardbred trotter, has acquired a subconscious nerve control, or reflex, that puts the pads down where they do the most good.

As the pad marks converge, *the fore and hind legs are carried straight forward in traveling, the stifles not turned inward or outward.* The inward angle of the leg is not produced by twisting the elbow and hock outward or the dog "moves out at the elbow" and/or "spread hocked."

FRONT LEG MOVEMENT

In the front leg, the angle starts at the shoulder point and the entire leg swings inward retaining the straight set of elbow, pastern, and phalanges. Viewed from the front, the leg forms a straight line, all parts moving in the same plane, from shoulder point to the base of the vertical center of gravity or a location approaching that center. Interference of the thoracic or rib structure on some dogs may cause a break at the elbow. Though the elbow still moves close to the body and in the same longitudinal plane, the degree of this break determines the effect on the efficiency of the gait, for the more it is out of line the greater will be the fatigue generated.

If the pad moves inward simply by the rotation of the ball and socket of the shoulder joint which in turn directs the elbow outward from the body, the dog is truely "moving out at the elbow." The leg action then is not in a longitudinal plane parallel with the line of locomotion but at an angle to it. Some dogs seem to do this deliberately, without the body structure prognosticating it, which may be their defense against the force of lateral displacement. Both actions hasten fatigue and lower the efficiency of the gait.

In some of the short-legged varieties of dogs, complete single-tracking cannot be obtained without forcing the elbows out. They will arrive at their most efficient locomotion with the least resultant fatigue by moving the pad marks inward, as far as possible, toward the center without breaking the straight line of the upper and lower arm or taking the leg action from a plane that is parallel with the line of locomotion. This will be governed by the roundness of ribs, by the height on the body at which the shoulder assembly is set, and particularly by the shape of the brisket or lower section of the thoracic walls.

The single-tracker will not strike his right leg with the left as one might expect even though both pads are moving forward on or above the line of locomotion. The pad is picked up off the ground and passes the opposite leg at a point where the angle of the leg removes it as an obstruction. Sometimes it may appear that the moving pad swings around the stationary one but this is often an optical illusion created by movement and is usually more pronounced in the back than front legs.

Sometimes features generally considered "deformities" are mechanical advantages for certain purposes. The majority of really good dancers are knocked-kneed. It is almost a characteristic for fast Standardbred trotters to have turned-out or slue front feet. The dog can rotate the back leg somewhat but he lacks that muscle which enables us to rotate our forearm.

The pad is more efficient if it is placed on the ground precisely in line with the direction of locomotion. Though we would like to see the entire leg action come in a plane parallel with this direction, that cannot always be the case. The front pad that is turned out slightly is more apt to leave a mark on the dust in line with this direction. This is probably a greater advantage to trotters and pacers than to gallopers, which accounts for the fact that we see it in the former more often than the latter when we visit race tracks.

BACK LEG MOVEMENT

In the back legs the inward angle starts at the stifle or the pelvic joint. Much that has been said about the front leg applies here also. The true action must not come from turned-out hocks which thus direct the pad toward the center and apply force at an angle to the line of progress. The leg must retain the original straight line as seen from the rear when standing true, with hocks neither in nor out, and it should move in a plane parallel with the line of locomotion. *This plane should run in a straight line from pelvic joint to pad mark, the latter being as close to the vertical center of gravity as possible.*

Stifles turning outward can come from a steep croup, short upper thigh or cow-hocks. This condition breaks the straight line of support and requires more muscular effort to maintain weight and motion.

Optical illusion may sometimes lead you to think that the dog is turning his hocks outward. They are moving on the outside of the pads because of the inclined angle of the leg which tends to throw your eye off as to their true position. A good ground coverer may have a tendency to turn the hocks slightly inward as he rotates the back pad to place it along the line of progress, and appear cow-hocked. However, like the slue-foot, if the leg is operating in a true plane from pelvis to pad mark, this is not necessary.

In many cases, though, *cow-hocks* are a mechanical advantage. Quite a number of great stake horses have been cow-hocked. Oxen, weight for weight, can out pull horses and they are decidedly cow-hocked. These are more or less the exception; they gain their advantage by off-setting some other feature which otherwise would be a hindrance in action.

AN EXPERIMENT IN BALANCE

You can run a table experiment to gain a clearer understanding of the value in single-tracking. Get a thin board about two inches wide and four inches long, or something else of the same character, along with four lathing nails or flat-headed screws. Draw a diagonal line from corner to corner of the block and one from end to end bisecting it equally.

The points of the four nails, thrust slightly into the wood at the four corners and on the diagonal line, will serve as do the four legs of the dog not in motion. Designate front and rear.

First we will consider the trot, which is a series of diagonals. Remove the left rear and the right front nails and you have the body support of the left diagonal. Note the difficulty in balancing the board on these two nails and particularly the rolling action which it suggests the body must go through in obtaining a balance.

Next, remove these nails and place them in the front and back end of the board on the center line. You will find it slightly easier to balance and note that the roll, when not in balance, is from right to left, and not at diagonals to the line of motion, which would set up more resistance.

Replace the left front nail and then insert one at the intersection of the two diagonals. Hold the board by the right rear corner so that it pivots on the center nail and so the front nail just barely touches the table. When you push on the right rear corner, as though the back leg were delivering power in a straight line along the side of the body, you can slide the board forward on the center nail; but it has a decided tendency to rotate to the left indicating the force which the left front leg must overcome and which is in addition to true lateral displacement. You can use a measured push and mark the arc described by the front leg.

Apply that same push to the board at and along the center bisector and you do not have any tendency to rotate, getting full travel without setting up transactive forces.

While we used the trot to illustrate this, the same forces exist in all gaits from the slowest walk to the fastest gallop, and they must be counteracted and corrected by the dog's legs whether he uses three of them or one of them to do it.

Lateral displacement and other transactive forces cannot be eliminated; they can only be reduced in their effect by the action and conformation of the dog. This summarizes down to a narrow base of support, as narrow as possible for the breed involved, an approach to or accomplishment of single-tracking, and the application of power along the line of progress.

In applying the force of the leg, whether the back with its major drive or the front working with or applying power, the foot itself should be placed on the ground so that its center line is on or parallel to the direction of progress. Neither the dog nor the horse can rotate the legs as readily as we do our forearms for the muscles that

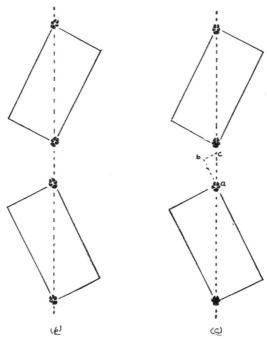

(b)   (c)

In projection "b" showing two diagonals
of the trot with pads on the line of progress,
the legs are traveling with body line and
therefore applying force at an angle to the
travel line. The legs are not carried straight
forward. The mathematical loss is in ratio
to the angle set up at the intersection with
the line of travel. Projection "c" shows the
same body condition solely for comparison
but with the pads traveling in line with that
of progress. The small triangle a-b-c establishes the value of the slightly turned out
front foot; the degree of its rotation depends upon the deviation from the travel line
that the leg itself takes. A dog traveling as
indicated here does carry his legs straight
forward and in related not counter planes.

do this are not as highly developed. The dog can rotate the back leg better than the front by swinging it in the hip socket.

Quite a number of fast trotters have their front hoofs slightly turned out or what dog breeders often call *east and west feet*. This may be a definite advantage and then again it may be a fault, and they are good trotters despite it.

It is when the dog has to rotate the upper and lower arm in the shoulder socket rather than swing it inward to get his pads under him that the turned out or slue foot is an advantage. The value of this as well as the action along the line of locomotion can be plotted mathematically.

The body is still a rectangle as the forces generated by the four legs originate at shoulders and hips which points establish the four corners of the rectangle. No matter how smoothly the dog is traveling there is a certain amount of body swing; when this is exaggerated the trot, for instance, will give us a rectangle inclined to the left when the right diagonal hits and to the right with the left diagonal; even not magnified the force is there to a degree.

The dog which has slightly turned out front feet—east and west or slue feet—does get them on the line of progress as his pad tracks on the ground indicate. An exaggerated slue though cannot be recommended. The same dog will be inclined to rotate the back leg, turning his pads inward as related to the body so that they fall on the line of progress. Therefore, when you watch the dog single-track he may appear to be moving with the hocks turned out.

Earlier in this chapter we indicated that cow-hocks could at times be a mechanical advantage. By the projection of these rectangles on the line of progress, we see the definite disadvantage to good locomotion for, even though the dog rotates the back leg some, he cannot make cow-hocks bring the pad on the travel line or even move in its plane.

Summarizing we can say that a good traveler puts the pads on or near the line of progress and keeps all four moving in planes which parallel this line.

8

Applied Anatomy

MOVEMENT in a dog is produced by the leverage action on the bones, the power applied by muscles, the latter attached to other bones so that you find both foundational and active members in the skeleton of the dog. The study of this will lead naturally to a consideration of anatomy.

"Anatomy!" your thoughts impetuously interrupt. "That's for the veterinarian to worry about. Who wants to wade through a lot of anatomical names!"

Yes, anatomy is for the veterinarian to worry about from a repair angle but it's your worry from the standpoint of function—what a given part is and does, and what makes it do the trick. We should know not so much the names but the relation of one bone to another and the attachments of the muscles so as to appreciate the effect that the movement of one part has upon another.

Beneath the pile of the Collie or the sleek coat of the Whippet, behind the tapering nose of the Borzoi or the lay-back of the Bulldog, bone and muscle structure is the same. Size may change but not numerical count, relation and function. A short back and loin has the same number of vertebrae as a long back and loin. So we can forget breed in the study of *applied anatomy*.

Bones, the tools with which the muscles of the dog work, must receive our first consideration. However, there is one item which we might sandwich in at this time consisting of both bone and content—the skull and brain.

There has always been controversy about the shape of the skull and its effect on the brain. Now, we are not interesting ourselves in a dog's ability to reason, so do not expect that tangent. Even so, science has not shown us that a wide brain is any more effective than a long, narrow one. There is a definite relation, insofar as natural intellect is shown, between the total size of the brain and

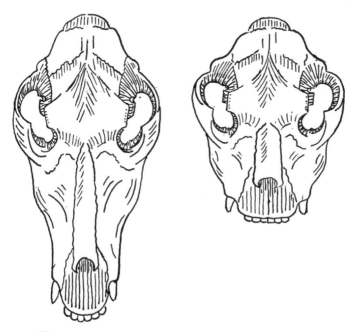

The dog's skull differs in outline with various breeds. The skull of a Greyhound and Boston, scaled to the same width, show that the major variation is in front of the eyes and does not affect brain capacity.

the relative size of the body but this does not mean that a 150-pound man wearing a number eight hat is more intellectual than one of equal size wearing a number seven hat. Also there appears to be some connection between the size of the spinal cord and instinct; and this influence may not always be located in the brain, for a chicken with head completely removed will live if the windpipe is kept open, the animal force-fed and prevented from bleeding to death.

The brain has three parts: the *medulla* which controls breathing is in the rear at the union with the spinal cord; the *cerebellum* in the mid-section reacts to reflexes and coordinates muscular action; and the *cerebrum,* located in the front, has to do with intellect. There are two parts, whether the dog thinks or not, which must be well developed—the *medulla* and *cerebellum*—that is all we have to say on that phase of the subject.

The skeleton of the dog, for our purpose, can be divided into three sections: the body, the front leg assemblies and the back leg assemblies. Of the first, the skull, vertebral column, ribs and sternum form the bone structure.

THE SKELETON OF THE BODY

The vertebral column is divided into five sections: neck, withers, back, loin and croup. To this we might add the tail, for it is a continuation of this column.

In the neck, we find seven vertebrae (cervical) regardless of breed and it is the first two of these that get our attention. They differ in shape from the others and allow free movement of the head. The point of their union with the other five divides the neck into two parts with separate sets of muscles attached to the parts. This union is usually distinctly shown by a pronounced bend in the arch of the back neck line—*it is the pole of the neck.*

The withers and back vertebrae (dorsal), numbering 13, have sockets in which the heads of the ribs rotate. The eight composing the withers have the longest vertical spires of all to provide anchorage for the shoulder muscles, *the span of which designates the withers.* The five vertebrae that make up the back show a gradual change in shape from the dorsal to those of the loin (lumbar) which have large transverse prongs and number seven in all. *Note that the anatomical back has but five vertebrae for* this will come up later in the specific study of the body.

The croup has three vertebrae (sacral) which are fused together to give a firm anchorage to the pelvis. The number of tail vertebrae (cocygeal) varies from five to 22 for they are the first to reveal mutation.

The heart and lungs are housed between 13 pairs of ribs. The latter have a bony section extending about two-thirds the full rib arc and articulate on the dorsal verte-

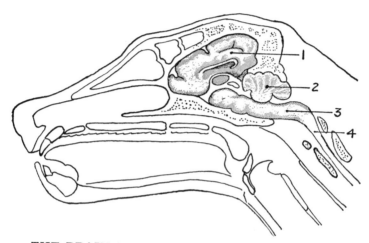

THE BRAIN is divided into three parts—1) The Cerebrum is the largest section, located in the crown of the skull, and though a mass of various nerve fibers, has a direct relation to the individual's ability to rationalize which might be called intelligence. This has a right and left lobe. 2) The Cerebellum is smaller and fits against the base of the skull below the occipital section; here, where reflexes are controlled and muscular action is coordinated, are the foundations of all training given to dogs. 3) The Medulla acts as the union between the two first parts and the spinal column, and through it pass all the nerve fibers. Some of these pass over to the opposite side of the cord, which accounts for the fact that one side of the brain controls certain actions on the opposite side of the body. This section is the seat of origin of some of the most important nerves of the body, including those of respiration. 4) The Spinal Cord is a cylindrical mass of nerves extending from head to sacrum. Tests indicate that its related size to body has a direct bearing on the animal's intelligence.

brae at the head, and a costal cartilage which attaches its lower end to the sternum or breast-bone in the case of the first nine and to the rib forward for the next four. The last pair is often unattached below the bone section.

BONES OF THE FRONT LEG

The front assembly is founded on the shoulder blade (scapula), of flat, triangular shape with a spine or ridge down the outer surface to provide muscle attachment. An oval cavity in the lower end receives the ball-like head of the upper arm at the point of the shoulder.

The upper arm (humerus) is a slender bone with a slight spiral twist, extending from the shoulder blade downward and backward in various degrees and lengths depending on the breed. In all, the general shape remains the same and the union with the shoulder blade is such that the opening of the angle between them is limited by a knob-like protrusion on the head of the upper arm. This has a definite influence on the function of the upper arm in movement.

The forearm consists of two bones (the radius in front and the ulna behind) and enters the structure at the elbow. The lower end of the upper arm which is round rests in a depression atop the radius bone; its round head has a groove in the back side into which the ulna fits and slides to provide the leverage action of the joint.

The pastern, at the lower end of the forearm, is made up of a number of small bones (carpal). The radius rests on a large radio-carpal in the front of the group. The most important bone here is the pisiform, L-shaped, with the short arm resting atop a metacarpal and the long arm extending backward. Near the mid-point of the latter rests the tip of the ulna so that the muscular action applied to the end of the pisiform manipulates both bones and puts the zip in pad action.

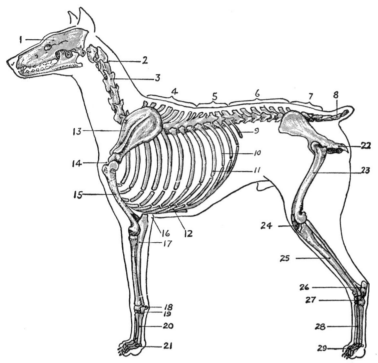

THE SKELETON of the dog, as we study it, consists of two groups: axial and appendicular. In the axial, we have: 1) Skull fitted to neck by ball and socket joint; 2) the Pole joint behind first two vertebrae; 3) seven vertebrae of the Neck; 4) eight vertebrae of the Withers; 5) five vertebrae of the Back; 6) seven vertebrae of the Loin; 7) three fused vertebrae of the Croup; 8) three to twenty-six vertebrae of the Tail; 9) one pair Floating Ribs; 10) three pairs Asternal Ribs joining each other at base; 11) nine Sternal Ribs connected to sternum by an intermediate cartilage section; 12) the Sternum or breast bone. In the appendicular, we have: 13) Shoulder Blade, scapula; 14) ball and socket joint at Shoulder Point; 15) Upper Arm, humerus; 16) Elbow, tip of ulna; 17) Fore Arm, radius and ulna; 18) Pisiform; 19) seven bones of Pastern Joint; 20) five metacarpals, only four active, forming Pastern; 21) phalanges forming four Toes; 22) Pelvis; 23) Upper Thigh, femur; 24) Knee Cap or Patella; 25) Lower Thigh, tibia and fibula; 26) Os Calcis; 27) five bones forming the Tarsal or Hock Joint; 28) five, four active, metatarsal bones forming Hock; 29) phalanges forming four Toes. The inactive metacarpal and metatarsal bones terminate into Dew Claws on the inside of each leg.

Below the pastern there are four metacarpal bones, long and slender, like those in the back of our hand between wrist and fingers. There is a fifth but it is not active in support. The dog's foot is made up of four digits, composed of three small bones to each digit, corresponding to those that make up our fingers.

BONES OF THE BACK LEG

The pelvis, a cage-like foundation of the back leg, is made up of three bones fused together on each side and laced to the spinal column where it forms the croup

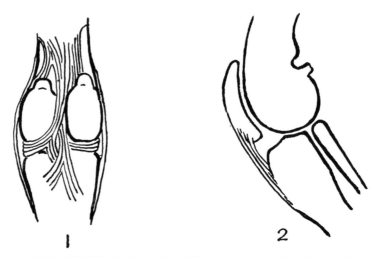

1   2

THE KNEE CAP or PATELLA forms a bearing surface against the muscles passing over it to the lower thigh against which the knob of the upper thigh rides when the stifle joint is moved. Sketch 1 indicates how the upper thigh is bound to the front bone (tibia) of the lower thigh by strands of ligaments. Sketch 2 is a sectional view of the Patella which should ride in the grooves formed by the knobs of the upper thigh. It has a flexible attachment by ligaments only to the lower thigh. If the binding muscles passing over it to the lower thigh are slack or the grooves poorly formed in the upper thigh, this has a tendency to slip out of place and cause lameness until it becomes reset.

(sacrum vertebrae). The thigh bone (femur) is attached to the pelvis by a ball and socket joint which provides free movement forward and back. The thigh or femur extends downward and forward to terminate in the stifle joint which has several interesting features. Here we have a round head resting on top of one bone while its curvature applies a push to another. We find also a knee-cap (patella) in front to prevent complete opening or straightening of the joint, and a knob on the back surface to check the movement in that direction.

The knee-cap (patella) should get careful consideration by all breeders, especially those of medium and small-size dogs, as so many have trouble with this part. The cap, very similar to the one in the human knee, is held in place by a single ligament and slides in a groove on the face of the lower end of the thigh bone. If this groove is not well developed there is little to prevent a slipped knee-cap which, until it is replaced and heals, puts the stifle out of commission. Small varieties do not have the groove proportionately developed and if excessively active are subject to this trouble.

Between the stifle and hock are two bones (tibia and fibula) that may fuse at the lower end in old dogs. This is often called the lower thigh.

The hock assembly (tarsus) is made up of seven bones, the most important of which is the *os calcis,* a long bone seated on the fourth tarsal and extending up to the hock point. While the tibia rests on one of the front bones of the assembly, the fibula seats on the *os calcis* so that it receives a leverage action when the point of the *os calcis* is manipulated.

Quadrupeds are all relatively the same in bone structure for which reason we run into many comparisons, especially with horses. The dog's structure also is not so unlike that of his master's. Often this has caused confusion or misconception and warrants putting the two side by side with the dog to bring out the contrast.

DOG SKELETON SIMILAR TO MAN'S

There is a legend told in the rough hills of northern India about two princes who grew up within the walls of their father's castle. The older had two great passions: love of adventure, and love for his brother over whom he watched as jealously as a she-leopard might her young. One day, the elder set out to seek greater adventures beyond his homeland.

Several years passed, during which time the father died and the younger brother acted as king, awaiting the rightful heir's return. Needless to say, the boy liked the job and wanted to keep it, so when word came that his brother was on his way home, he bargained with an old witch to do away with the man.

Days later a strange animal made its way into the castle but as it showed only affection for the king it was not destroyed. It was into this animal that the witch had changed the older brother and they called it a dog, supposedly the first of the species. The second one was created when a girl who had loved the older brother discovered what had happened to him and begged the witch to change her into a dog also. Thereafter the two of them repaid the treachery with the faithfulness and attachment which has always marked this animal's attitude toward man.

A fantastic story, but as we examine the dog's skeleton we find much that might have given rise to it. The dog's front leg has the same group of bones found in man's arm except that the dog's shoulder blade is relatively larger and is placed on the side of the thoracic section, and the humerus or upper arm is relatively shorter so that the elbow is nearer the sternum line.

The dog's pastern corresponds to the human's wrists; his front foot is made up of the same bones found in a man's fingers with the heel that section of the palm at finger union. Thus the dog walks on his fingers in front. In the back leg, much like his owner's leg, the femur is

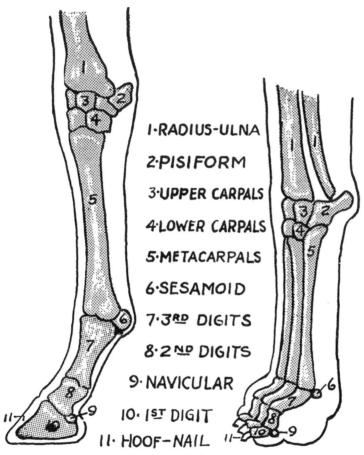

1·RADIUS-ULNA

2·PISIFORM

3·UPPER CARPALS

4·LOWER CARPALS

5·METACARPALS

6·SESAMOID

7·3ᴿᴰ DIGITS

8·2ᴺᴰ DIGITS

9·NAVICULAR

10· 1ˢᵀ DIGIT

11· HOOF-NAIL

The front legs of a horse and dog are similar in a general way, having identically the same basic bones. A comparison shows that the horse's knee is the same as the dog's pastern joint, while the bones forming the horse's pastern are actually in the dog's foot.

relatively shorter and the dog walks on four toes with his hock corresponding to man's heel and ankle joint.

HORSE AND DOG COMPARED

"You never see a horse with straight pasterns," we have heard many say, especially an eminent British writer on canine topics, "so why put them on dogs. It's like walking around on sticks."

What these people may have failed to realize is that a horse's knee, in his front leg, is the same joint that we designate as a dog's pastern. The bones which form the horse's pastern are the second and third digits and are found in the dog's foot. The horse probably never lived with pastern slope equal to that which the dog has in the same bones.

Horsemen do not like a horse's knee to bend backward as does a dog's pastern; they term him *calf-kneed*. To a horse, its only advantage is sure-footedness over rough ground; at the same time it reduces weight-carrying ability and puts too much strain on ligaments and muscles.

In dogs, we must consider other angles. He does not have to carry weight other than that of his own body and if he is even one-twentieth the size of a horse he will find any given terrain approximately 20 times rougher than does the horse. The sloping pastern will add comparative length to the extended leg and in many front assemblies is necessary to bring the pad under the vertical center of gravity. So the two problems are not identical.

It should also be noted that the dog has a much better developed pisiform bone which makes his pastern more amiable to muscle control and offsets many of the disadvantages that a horse might experience with a calf-knee.

BONE SIZE AND TEXTURE

Bone relation has always been persistent in following the norm that nature sets up as her desire rather than the breeder's. For instance, if we want a short humerus or upper arm while still retaining the long, well laid-back shoulder blade, the latter tends to shorten with the former. All bones are predisposed to a normal balance with one another and will follow or return to this if given but half a chance.

Left alone for several generations, almost any strain of Fox Terrier will either go short headed or take on a larger body and longer legs to match the head. This tendency was quite evident at the peak of this dog's popularity when many kennels persisted in breeding among their own dogs only. The small shoulder blade so often seen on these dogs is a result of an attempt to conform to the short upper arm. The excess length over height found and desired in German Shepherds would soon be lost if the breeders become negligent for but a short span. What is true of these breeds is true of others for it is a persistent law of nature to make parts match according to her own pattern.

Bones are composed of both animal and mineral matter in such an intricate blending that we can remove the animal matter by heat or the mineral by acid without disturbing the other, and the form of the bone will remain the same until compression or jar changes it. However, without both elements, the bone has no strength.

The texture of the bone, which has far more to do with its strength than does its size, is apparently affected by heredity, feeding and age or sickness. In the latter case anything which depletes the natural calcium supply of the system will then begin to take it from the bones themselves leaving more or less a shell.

There was an old saying regarding human mothers,

"A tooth for every child." While this need not be true, it was based on the fact that if the natural storage and intestinal supply of calcium is not sufficient for the demand the mineral will be extracted from other available sources. Bitches carrying and nursing puppies will go off in bone texture if not properly fed. Age will open up the texture and make the bone brittle as will high fevers, over exertion, and particularly neurotic disturbances.

Proper food quite naturally works in the reverse by supplying bone building material. Bone is built from calcium and phosphorus activated into union by vitamin D. At this writing, we are not positive but there is much to indicate that vitamins A and C do influence texture and quality. There is one definite fact, however, in regard to food and bones: *you cannot feed more bone into a dog than his natural heritage prescribes,* you can only insure that he develops that heritage. As the dog lives and works, you can maintain his bone quality by proper food.

By emphasis, we might add that there is more to the production of bone from food than the presence of the minerals and vitamins just mentioned. There are all the other factors of metabolism—the energy-yielding process essential to life, by which a living cell of the dog transforms food material into its own protoplasm; in other words, the many other factors that make the machine work toward good health in general.

It is our advice to place bone health far above apparent size when judging the quality of these bars that jack the dog around and house the mechanism of his body. All individual bones of the skeleton are joined and held by a softer material known as ligament and cartilage and these are of quality and texture relative with the bone.

There are thousands of illustrations bearing out bone quality over size but none more emphatic than once stood almost side by side in the bluegrass meadows of Kentucky—two stallions which had retired to that manner of living which any man might envy.

"What a magnificent animal!" exclaimed a visitor who had approved the expenditure of thousands of dollars for good horse flesh as he gazed in open-faced admiration on one of these horses. "Look at the bone and legs under that fellow—the best I've—"

"Never saw better bone in my life in any horse's legs," his companion involuntarily commended.

"If you think those are good bones and legs, I want you to see another stallion just down the road," said the commission buyer who accompanied them.

A few minutes later they breasted the white board fence of a neighboring paddock as four small hoofs beat a tattoo across the green drum head.

"That . . ." and you hardly knew whether it was an exclamation or question.

"He looks like a big potato with toothpicks stuck in it!"

"Exactly," agreed the trained buyer, "but they had to weight that horse off the track, his legs still sound; and he's putting sound legs on his progeny. The other—he was off the track at four and none of his get's done any better—bad legs."

No wise horse buyer ever rates quality of bone by its size and we can find no scientific reason for considering dogs as an exception to this fact.

In performing autopsies, we have often cut through the bones to examine the cross section. The observations made can be listed as follows: large bones of a given breed are more porous than normal; small bones present a denser construction; the exterior of the large bone when polished tends to have pits while the small bone takes a higher polish; cross sectional strength is relatively the same.

That applies to animals which have died in good health and which are about the same age. Any animal which has suffered a prolonged illness, especially with high fever, shows the effect of it in the cross-section texture of its bones. The bones still have their shape but they have gone through pretty much the same treatment mentioned when we suggested removing the mineral and animal matter with acid and heat.

BONE AND DISPOSITION

Observation also tends to show a linkage between bone size and the disposition of the dog, or perhaps we should say nervous energy and reflexive action. Watch closely the dispositions of the small boned, finely drawn specimens of any given breed and you will find that they more often have the "guts" or intestinal fortitude to keep right on going, right on fighting—they are the "do or die" fellows. On the other hand, you will find more shy specimens among them as a group. Heavy-boned individuals are quite likely endowed with a happy-go-lucky disposition, not given much to displaying an abundance of energy; they are steady, less apt to be shy whether of gun or strangers and are not as inclined to bite. These particular facts have been carefully watched by a veterinarian who has handled personally far more than 100,000 dogs.

Regardless of whether they are good or bad, fine grained or porous and spongy, the bones are the framework of the dog's body and the instruments or tools with which his muscles must work in moving him about. They must be considered in that respect when judging the dog.

9

The Muscles in Use

EVEN as the doctor might feel the patient's pulse before deciding what ailment to expect, we can examine the dog's muscles for an idea as to his expected performance, for they are the power and force that put motion in locomotion. From our angle, we are not particularly interested in the anatomic names and specific boundaries of these muscles except as they create a direct effect. In discussing them we shall consider them in groups that do a particular job, such as draw the front leg forward or straighten the back leg, in short, their functions.

Muscles are fleshy, elastic bands activated by nerves so that they contract and elongate and, by so doing, move the bones to which they are attached. Their actual shape and means of attachment varies with the purpose and location. They have two parts: the red, fleshy part which is active; the white tendinous part, slightly elastic but inactive, which forms the attachments either immediately or through cords running to distant members of the frame.

As a dog grows older, more and more of the fleshy part turns to tendinous which accounts for the fact that age reduces activity. Nature may choose that course to prevent an old boy from over-taxing a wornout heart and brittle bones. Whatever the reason there is less proportionate active muscle on an old dog than was there when he was a young scamp.

MUSCLE FUNCTION

Science has shown us that a muscle will contract two-thirds the length of the fleshy part. A muscle with six inches of unattached flesh will contract four inches, while three inches of the former will give us but two inches in action. Therefore, if we are interested in the action of a certain part we must strive to increase the actual length of the fleshy part of the muscle that operates it.

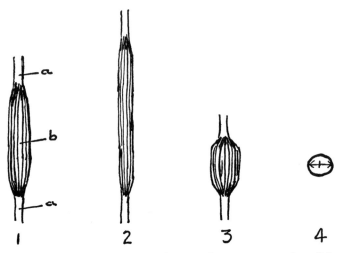

A muscle is composed of an active center section (b) terminating in inactive tendinous fibers (a). The active part contracts two-thirds its length but normally rests in semi-contracted condition as it opposes some other muscle in maintaining balance as shown in sketch 1. Sketch 2 compares full extension as the opposing muscle contracts, while sketch 3 shows the same muscle fully contracted. As indicated at 4, strength is related to cross-section but by no means is always dependent on it.

It has also been established that a broad, heavy muscle will not respond to reflexive action as quickly as a smaller one of the same length. Nor does the latter burn up as much energy in doing its job. Thus building heavy muscles will curtail initial speed and reflexive response, though it does add to strength. To this fact is probably due the adage, "A slim horse for a long race."

The three main facts for us to remember about muscles

are: the fleshy part is active, tendons non-active; action is in ratio to length; strength is derived from cross section area or size.

The length of a muscle is quite naturally dependent on the distance between origin and terminus, so a long bone indicates a long muscle. With nature's idea of balancing things, we find that muscles and bones usually run hand-in-hand as regards size; large bones are accompanied by large muscles, small or fine bones have them cut to their pattern.

When a specific breed or an individual of that breed is selected for heavy bone, you can expect the muscles to be coarse in texture, comparatively slow in action, quicker to tire but with relatively more applied strength. The light, fine-boned individual of the same breed should have close textured muscles that respond to reflexes more quickly, show more agility and endurance but lack the applied strength. An extreme in the former case will usually be sloppy and lazy, in the latter case weak and neurotic.

The normal condition of a muscle when apparently dormant is "in tension" or at least in half-tension. This is because one set or muscle works against others to retain a member in balance, then when the member moves one of these has contracted further while the other has extended or relaxed. Actually there is a definite tension on all of them regardless of the position of the member or it would not remain firmly in place.

We have probably had friends who after a cold or chill had one side of their face twist into a contorted condition. The side to which the face was drawn was not due to the muscles on that side becoming more tense but to those on the uncontorted side relaxing and refusing to remain in tension. All muscles activating a given member such as the shoulder blade must remain in balance and coordinate with one another in every movement of the blade.

As you study the various sets of muscles, we believe you will agree that their application sets up some very interesting engineering feats. Nature did a right smart job and certainly knew how to make the most use of a given force.

The head has a number of muscles but only two of them are interesting to us from a service application: the two biting muscles. The major one (masseter) is fastened to the lower jaw just in front of the socket and to the upper skull above the back teeth where it spreads out fan-

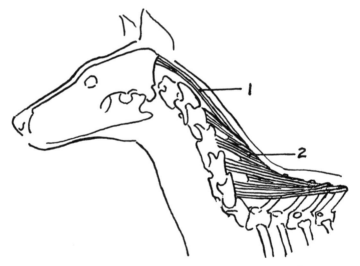

THE CERVICAL LIGAMENT is the most important factor in the efficiency of the Neck. It has (1) a strong cord running from the occipital point of the skull to the fourth dorsal vertebra. Hanging to this, like a tent over a ridge pole, is another part (2) which fans out and attaches to the four vertebrae below the Pole of the Neck. This ligament controls the position of the head and is the basic strength to the forward action of the leg as it bears the weight of that muscular action.

shaped. It possesses more power than any other head muscle. The other one (zygomaticus) is a long strip extending from the cartilage of the ear to the front of the lower jaw. Its main mission is to retract the jaw but it comes into service on the bite particularly for long-headed dogs.

Though the muscles on the neck are more interesting to us because of their activation of the front leg assembly, there is a ligament there which should have our attention —the *suspensory* or *cervical ligament,* and unlike other ligaments it does have reflexive stretch and retraction. This remarkable, elastic apparatus supports the long neck and head, governs head carriage, and stabilizes the base attachments of the muscles that move the leg forward and that rotate the crown of the shoulder blade forward as the leg moves backward.

This ligament is divided into two parts. The first is a cord running along the top of it from the base of the skull to the fourth dorsal vertebra where it becomes a part of the spinal ligaments. The second part is a web or sheet running back from all neck vertebrae, except the first two, to this cord and the spires of the dorsal vertebrae.

You will note that only the cord is attached beyond the first two vertebrae of the neck. It is the juncture of these two vertebrae with the others of the neck that is designated as the "pole," and usually shows as a more definite break in the neck line. The main body of this muscle is attached to the remainder of the neck vertebrae. The former section carries the terminals of the muscles that move the foreleg forward or lift it; the latter section supports the front muscles of the shoulder blade.

It is quite important that this ligament be strong and well anchored on long spires or large vertebrae, a fact which will quickly be appreciated when we note the tax put on it by the movement of the front limb. The ewe neck does not have a good ligament.

MUSCLES OF THE SHOULDER

The top of the shoulder blade is mainly supported and cushioned between two flat muscles, which are triangular or fan shaped, one above (trapezius) and one below (rhomboideus) the blade. What we say of one applies to the other. While the muscle on top of the blade has the same name fore and aft, it really functions as two muscles. It is attached in the center, and at its widest part, to the ridge running down the blade. The forward portion is attached to the first vertebra of the withers and the ligament of the neck, transmitting most of its burden to the latter. The back portion is attached to the dorsal muscle and the second to the eighth vertebra. It is the span of this muscle which limits the withers and marks the point where the anatomical back begins. In action it lifts the blade or rotates it forward and backward according to which span is contracting.

The lower part of the blade is carried in a wide muscular band (serratus) which also functions in two halves, the forward portion operating from the ridge of the blade upward to put its burden on the neck ligament, the after part fanning out broader and attaching itself to several ribs back to the eighth one. When the leg moves forward, the point of the shoulder blade rotates in that direction; the back part of the trapezius and the front portion of the serratus doing most of the work.

The shoulder blade does not pass the shock of concussion to its sustaining muscles in a straight line along its center as though these muscles were considered a pocket. If it did, the result would be the same as if a baseball player caught a hard-thrown ball without allowing his glove to give with the force of the ball, and the resultant shock would be several times greater than the shoulder action allows it to be.

The force of the shock when the ground is contacted comes up the forearm and upper arm to the shoulder point. At this instant, the point of the shoulder blade rotates around the center of the blade upward or more precisely forward although it will have to move in the opposite direction while completing the stride. The muscles which take this first shock are the upper front and lower rear

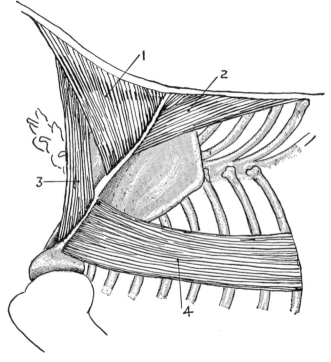

The muscles of the Shoulder Blade can be understood by a study of two sets. The top of the blade is held by the Trapezius (1 and 2) which really is two muscles for the two halves oppose each other. Below this and of almost identical shape and action is the Rhomboideus. The lower half of the Blade has the Serratus (3 and 4) which likewise is divided as to parts and action. As the Blade rotates on its center in leg action, muscular section 1 coordinates with 4, 2 cordinates with 3 as to contraction and expansion.

of the group cushioning it. After the first initial impact, which they hold, they start the blade on its backward rotation where it is carried by momentum and the load is then transferred to the upper back and the lower front muscles. The blade continues to pivot on its center and

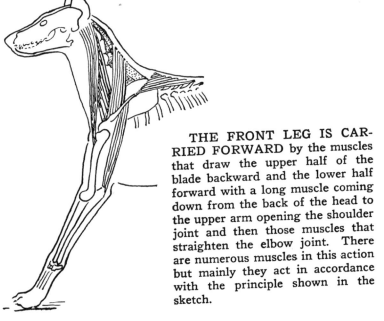

THE FRONT LEG IS CARRIED FORWARD by the muscles that draw the upper half of the blade backward and the lower half forward with a long muscle coming down from the back of the head to the upper arm opening the shoulder joint and then those muscles that straighten the elbow joint. There are numerous muscles in this action but mainly they act in accordance with the principle shown in the sketch.

these muscles take the load until the foot leaves the ground in the follow-through. After that the load is transferred back to the former muscles for the return of the leg. This is a rolling, riding action and very much reduces the force transmitted to the muscles. It can be likened to the baseball player letting his glove ride with the force of the ball.

Another important feature to leg action, which we might note here, is the follow-through. Every golfer and baseball player knows the value of a club or bat continuing along the same arc for a slight distance after it has contacted the ball. The same action is of value to the impulse applied by the leg.

The upper arm (humerus) is drawn forward primarily

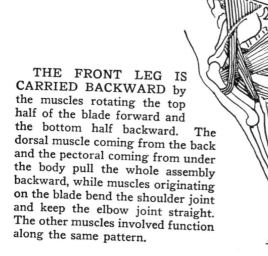

THE FRONT LEG IS CARRIED BACKWARD by the muscles rotating the top half of the blade forward and the bottom half backward. The dorsal muscle coming from the back and the pectoral coming from under the body pull the whole assembly backward, while muscles originating on the blade bend the shoulder joint and keep the elbow joint straight. The other muscles involved function along the same pattern.

by a very long, slender muscle (levator humeri) which originates beyond the pole of the neck at the base of the skull and terminates just below the shoulder joint on the upper arm. When the neck ligaments remain taut, it swings the upper arm forward; when these ligaments relax, the head is drawn downward if both muscles act, or to one side if only one of them contract. Throatiness and loose skin, except in the Bulldog or those breeding for this condition, indicate sloppy muscles in this section.

MUSCLES OF FRONT LEG

Bending the forearm at the elbow is done by a muscle (brachii) that has one attachment on the shoulder blade just above the joint, runs down in front of this and helps to hold the head of the upper arm in place, and attaches to the radius bone of the forearm. It not only bends the elbow joint but when the dog is not in motion opposes the muscles that bend the shoulder joint to stabilize the assembly. This muscle comes into extra play when the dog "pads" to avoid momentum shock. When the pad strikes the ground, the elbow should not be bent but remain as taut and straight as possible. Unless disturbed by the muscle just discussed, this is done mostly by the triceps, enormous, short, triangular muscles which originate on the top portion of the shoulder blade and are attached to the peak of the ulna at the elbow.

Originating around the elbow are several muscles which change to tendinous cords and which attach themselves to the pisiform of the pastern or to the digits. Their mission is to hold these joints and members tense and straight or bend the toes and pastern. To appreciate their action with that of the triceps, grasp the dog's leg firmly just above the elbow joint and extend it forward: the pastern and toes will straighten; slap them with the other hand and they will flick back into place immediately and automatically. The same action, taking place in the back leg, shows the tension under which they are when first striking the ground.

The backward movement of the leg entails more and rather complicated muscular action. The leg really does not move backward except when the dog is digging but the body moves forward over it. When contact comes with the ground, it is extended and straight but the first action is that of folding up or crumbling beneath the dog's body and then a restraightening or extending.

Shoulder blade rotation is accomplished by the front half of the trapezius acting on the top of the blade and the after band of the serratus drawing the lower half of the blade backward. The two other halves of these muscles are called upon to take the first shock and to stabilize the whole action by counterbalance.

The bending of the upper arm, humerus, at the shoulder joint must entail a lot of power for there are three major muscles doing the job assisted by quite a number of minor ones. Perhaps more complicated muscular action is applied to this movement than any other of the body. The main zip that comes into this is supplied by the great dorsal, the pectoral and the triceps; the auxiliaries are the various flexors of the upper arm originating on the blade and operating along the base of a triangle formed by the blade and upper arm.

MUSCLES OF THE BODY

The great dorsal (lastissimus dorsi) is a broad, triangular muscle which starts over the loins and the last four dorsal vertebrae; wrapping itself around the ribs it terminates in a tendon which is inserted into the head of the upper arm near the shoulder joint. This ripples on the dog's side as he moves.

The pectoral muscle starts along the sternum or underside of the rib structure and terminates in approximately the same place as the great dorsal. You will note that both of these muscles apply their action near the fulcrum putting strain on themselves but gettting more action at the elbow end of the bone.

The body has the most powerful and complex muscle of the whole structure in the long dorsal (longissimus dorsi) which extends along the spinal column from the pelvis to the neck. It is attached not only at these two ends but to the processes of all vertebrae between them. Its action might be likened somewhat to a caterpillar making a procession of itself along the floor.

This muscle may act on one side of the back line or on both at once; it gives a base support to the neck ligament and keeps the entire spinal column in its proper place and alignment. It is balanced and countered by a long muscle

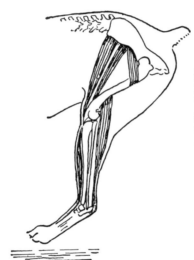

THE BACK LEG is carried forward by muscles coming from Pelvis to Upper and Lower Thighs drawing the Upper Thigh forward and straightening the Stifle Joint; muscles of the Lower Thigh bending the Hock Joint and opposed by a muscle from Upper Thigh to Os Calcis (Achilles tendon) to balance, tense and then straighten this joint.

band (psoas magnus) beneath the loin vertebrae. There are several muscles in the latter group which operate between the thigh and pelvis beneath the loins up to the last ribs—they arch the back and function in thigh action.

One of the most important muscles of the body is the diaphragm, a flat sheet separating the thoracic cavity from the abdominal, placed obliquely downward and forward, forming a wall between these two cavities. Its major mission is to control breathing but it is used also to raise the ribs and to promote expulsion from the colon.

MUSCLES OF THE BACK LEG

When the back leg is moved forward it must be lifted and then extended. The lift comes mostly from the muscles in front of the thigh joint, coming down from the pelvis to the upper thigh or femur. One is a strong thick tissue starting in front of the pelvis and extending to the lower end of the thigh (gluteus medius). There is an-

THE BACK LEG is drawn backward by the strongest muscles of the assembly. Powerful muscles come down from the Pelvis and Croup to the Lower Thigh; note the ingeniousness of the wrap-around which not only draws the Stifle Joint backward but straightens it. The Achilles tendon straightens the Hock Joint. The muscles of the Loin and Back also enter into this action and all those shown in the sketch are known as the rearing muscles.

other (profundus) running from the spine to approximately the same location on the thigh. A third (superficillis) comes over the crown of the croup to the lower end of the thigh bone.

The hock joint is straightened in this action and others by a muscle originating at the base and on the back of the thigh and running down to the *os calcis* or heel (gastrocnemius). This muscle becomes a long tendon, the Achilles tendon, before reaching the calcis, where it is fixed but has the ability to glide over the tip of the latter.

The back leg also contracts as its backward arc starts
and then is again straightened with a strong thrust. The
major muscles, which draw it backward, are those on the
back side of the thigh. One is a powerful tissue that

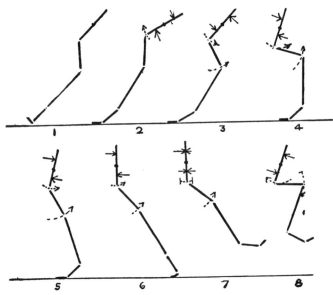

The complete back action of the leg is shown with
Shoulder Blade muscular reflex indicated by the dark
arrows that mark the face of the blade on which muscles are in tension or contracting. 2) Receiving first
concussion, movement of Shoulder Joint indicated by
broken arrow. 3) Direction of travel changes, moving
to the rear and continuing until position 7 where it is
momentarily static. Note the follow-through indicated
in this position. 8) The leg begins its return for another stride.

arises on the vertebrae of the croup (biceps femoris), is
attached to the back of the pelvis and then comes down
to the crown of the tibia, the larger of the bones below
the stifle joint. Just behind this and usually indicated
by a depression between the two is another muscle (semitendinosus) which runs from the back end of the pelvis

to the tibia. Their action is such that they not only draw the leg backward but tend to straighten the stifle joint.

The snap that is put into the drive of the back leg owes as much to muscles straightening the hock joint at this time as to those drawing the leg backward.

The final drive to the back leg is accomplished by a complete set of muscles known as the *rearing muscles*. These straighten the digits, the hock joint, the stifle joint and draw the leg backward; no less a part of them are the two dorsals, particularly the long dorsal.

MUSCLE TONE

As has been pointed out earlier in this discussion, muscle size is not as important as quality and this might mean the normal or healthy condition of the tissues or organ—tone.

One thing of which we can reasonably be certain is that, barring specific injury, the health or tone of one muscle is on a par with another in the same dog. Over the major activating muscles are thin layers of muscles and tissues which eventually attach themselves to the skin. Therefore muscle tone can be judged fairly accurately by skin tone, the keynote of *condition*.

Our dogs can profit by some of our own experience in condition. Following a period of inactivity our joints are stiff, muscles are slow to react, tendons have lost some of their elasticity and our whole muscular and nervous system fails to coordinate as it once did. Even professional athletes cannot function at the beginning of the season as they do in mid-season. So that brings us to the answer of action and exercise, plus good food, for muscle tone. Just as no dog can be any better than his bone placement and conformation, he can be no better than his muscle tone.

10

The Shoulder Blade

"Sixty miles by dawn?" questioned Tommy, the American engineer as he looked at the round, brown chin showing beneath the sloppy brimmed sombrero. "It's impossible!"

The chin moved slowly. "Nossing ees ven *he* geeves an order!"

Tommy sighed. He was about to get some practical experience in more things than how they conduct revolutions below the Rio Grande. Looking about him, he knew that the others were taking the marching order seriously for they had broken their siesta and were milling about getting their horses ready—a motley mass with worn charro dress and sturdy boots mingling with pajama-like dirty whites and brown feet showing through rope-tied sandals. Only two things seemed in uniform—the red and yellow blankets under which they hid from the chill of night and the broad brimmed hats under which they hid from the torrid heat of day.

The brown chin moved again. "Senor, you better not ride the golden one."

For several days, Tommy had been riding a beautiful palomino whose golden coat was made richer by contrast with his silver mane and tail. Not ride him—the thought was absurd; and Tommy said as much.

"He weel break your neck—you see."

"Huh—he's never tried to buck. Besides" . . . but the brown chin had turned away.

An hour later, they were on the trail that would snake through rough hills, shoot like an arrow across a broad mesa and then stagger into more hills. The early pace was slow, held to a walk or jog trot, and Tommy listened to the steady hum of voices and the rhythm of hoof beats punctuated by the clank of iron shoes on rocks. He smelled the clean sweet tang that belongs to horses with sweat-fringed girths and flecks of silver about bits, warm horses packed together in a mass.

When night came and the men were marked out by the glow of their cigarettes, the pace was increased; eventually it would become a steady canter. The fresh joy was now changing into one monotonous hour after another for Tommy and then—

Each cantering stride, as the palomino fought gamely to keep pace with the other horses, registered with him like the tick of an old alarm clock in the night. Remembering some of his old riding lessons, he kept shifting the lead, but the tick remained and grew louder. Finally it became an atrocious pain that shot up his spine and cracked at the base of his brain. The night grew darker and darker and then the pain ceased.

Tommy rolled over on the hard dirt floor, streaked by a single shaft of light, and groped to find his head. Looking up, he could see more than the little round chin, he could see the whole face with its half amused, half vindictive smile.

"Deed I not tell you, Senor, that palomino break your neck? You gringos know eet all, but you do not know how to peek a horse for a long ride."

"But how—" Tommy stammered still too stunned to feel embarrassed that he had passed out on the palomino.

The little brown man shrugged: "I show you."

He walked to the door whence came the streak of light and returned leading the buckskin which he had ridden through the night. Without the formality of a show ring pose, his stubby finger pointed.

"See thees—eet mus' rear back as man een a hammock," and he was indicating the shoulder blade. "The golden one's ees steef as a chair. And thees," he continued pointing to the fetlock, "eet mus' almos' keess the ground."

Whether Tommy knew it or not, in those words he received an education about the forequarters of a horse—about a dog as well—and maybe his experience did make him appreciate it. We cannot all learn the value of a well laid back shoulder blade that emphatically. Regrettable, for it might put us on the right track as a hairbrush curbs juvenile delinquency.

THE SHOULDER BLADE'S JOB

The forehand assembly of a dog is as busy as a centipede crossing the floor. For all dogs it has five missions and for terriers, six. First, it must support weight. Second, it must absorb concussion both from momentum of the gait and the jump. Third, it must propel on the turns. Fourth, there is lateral displacement to be off-set. Fifth, it must aid in or maintain the level of the center of gravity. Sixth, the terriers use it for spade and shovel. Remember that in every stride of every dog at least four of these are manifested.

This is a pretty fair assignment and the factors involved apply equally to the sheltered house pet and the "big going" field trial contender. As our dogs in general are not subjected to severe tests afield, the importance of the forehand often escapes us. Horsemen need no reminders, for they know that the majority of Thoroughbreds breaking down on the track do so in front. We are only kidding ourselves if we think our dogs are any sounder in this respect.

A Boston or other small dog jumping from your lap to floor receives more concussion relatively than a horse taking the bars in the Maryland Hunt Cup race. You may not think of your house dog as facing the problems of a field dog but if you hang a pedometer on his collar some-day you are in for a surprise.

The weight that the Chihuahua's shoulder supports is the same in proportion to that of a Dane's. In propelling on turns, lifting the center of gravity and countering

Thickening muscles beneath the Blade to gain strength forces the top outward, bringing the shoulder point in and the elbow out as indicated in this dog's right front assembly. Compared with this is the left assembly which provides a straight column of bones below the shoulder point for support. Strength must be acquired by other means than thickening muscles.

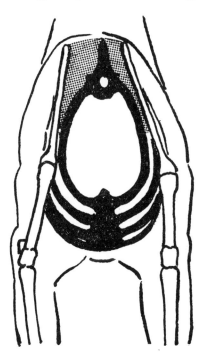

lateral displacement, the only difference between the little fellows on your rugs and hounds working a wolf's trail is that in the latter faults of gaits and endurance are easily measured against other hounds in the race. We may dodge the issue of the requirements of a good front but the dogs cannot.

The foundation of this front assembly is the shoulder blade and no structure can be better than its groundwork. Some standards ask for *long* and most of them for *sloping* or *well laid back* blades in recognition of and an effort to improve the blade set. These terms were probably synonyms in the originators' minds.

In analyzing the blade to arrive at the best answer for its placement, we must first consider its support. This, as was pointed out, is by muscles and tendons which act to rotate the blade approximately on its center. We also noted that the motility of a muscle was related to its length, and its strength to its cross-section area. So, the first question is: what blade gives us the longest muscles for motility and the largest for strength.

We might increase the thickness of the outside muscles without damage to the structure, but we cannot do the same with the corresponding muscles that lie beneath the blade. As muscles run hand-in-hand with one another, whatever we do to one will be reflected on the other. If the one beneath the blade is thickened, the blade will be pushed out at the top which will either widen the front or rotate the blade on the curve of the ribs, bringing the point in and turning the elbows out. This gives us "loaded shoulders," always a fault. The wide front has a clumsy battle with lateral displacement and the misplaced elbows disrupt the columnar support of the legs. Therefore, we must look to some other means of increasing the cross-section area and getting a larger, longer muscle.

SIXTY VERSUS FORTY-FIVE DEGREE BLADE

The portion of the body that can be allotted to the blade is limited because the upper arm must also be placed on the body area unless we choose to change the whole make-up of the dog. That is not the idea. The idea is to make the best of what we have and still keep the dog as he is in general appearance. However, the vertical height which can be assigned to the blade is relatively the same in all members of a given breed. That is, the space allotted on one Fox Terrier is comparative to that on another Fox Terrier. Therefore, we can take an arbitrary range and examine blades set at different angles within its scope to determine which is the most valuable.

With the height assumed, we can strike off a square for projecting this backward on the body so that it does not

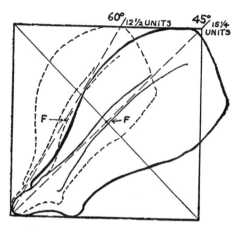

A 60- and 45-degree blade compared mathematically shows that the latter is 15¼ units long as against 12½ units, a gain of 22% in this feature, and also a gain in width of blade, which provides large muscles.

interfere with any of the dog's functions. On this square we can impose blades set at different angles and compare their size and efficiency.

We inscribe a blade set at 60 degrees to the ground line and one at 45 degrees. If the former measures 12½ units, the latter will measure 15¼ units in mid-line length. This is an increase of 38 per cent. Beyond the 45-degree angle, the value is lost as rapidly as gained up to that point. This longer blade will also be wider and carry a higher center ridge for muscular attachment.

Many standards must have the 45-degree blade in mind

although it is not so stated. The "sloping" or "long" and "long and sloping" can reach their maximum only at that degree. In other standards where the set of the upper arm is requested at 90 degrees to the blade, the latter would have to approach the 45-degree set unless the former courts a parallel line with the ground and give an

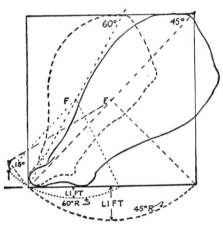

A Blade pivoting on its center describes an arc with its point. The
length of the arc establishes its value
in locomotion. The mechanical lift derived from it is governed by the dome
of the arc. In both of these factors,
the 45-degree blade is far superior to
the 60-degree blade.

assembly similar to an ox's which is certainly not what the Dobe or Dachs Standards intended.

As the front assembly must assist or actually do the re-lifting of the center of gravity, the effect of the blade on this mission is quite important. When the blade joins in a stride, the joint swings forward upwards of 15 degrees and then backwards throughout the stride. The useful part of the backward action is limited to the intersection with the horizontal level of the normal position. The useful arc of the 60-degree blade is but little more than half that of the 45-degree one from a purely mathematical and mechanical standpoint.

One of the most important factors involved here is the difference in the ability to lift. The 45-degree blade is approximately 2½ times more effective in this mission than the 60-degree blade. Write that in capital letters in your memory.

The vertical and horizontal boundary lines of the square on which we have imposed the shoulder blade can be assumed to represent the lines of force: there is a vertical and a horizontal force present at all times. These forces cannot be known for an individual application and they may not always be equal. However, the known factors applied to the shoulder blade tend to show them approximately so. The nearer the pivotal center of the blade falls on the intersections of the diagonals formed by these forces, the better will be the kinetic balance of the blade.

As noted in the illustration the 45-degree blade describes a much longer arc with its point than does the 60-degree blade. There is far more advantage to this than the increased distance of travel. Thrust to the front and lift derived from the entire leg action is derived when the front leg entirely straightens. In the short arc of the 60-degree blade this thrust is directed far more vertically than it is in the 45-degree blade, where the thrust is more along the line of body travel. This factor perhaps more than anything else accounts for the fact that dogs with "upright" shoulders resemble rocking horses going across the field—traveling upward as much as forward.

LEVERAGE AND STRIDE

The laws of leverage come galloping into this picture like tax collectors. From these laws we have learned that if the distance between P and F is increased without a change between *F* and *W* we reduce muscular effort and fatigue. You can look into the grab-bag for any set of muscles operating from this blade and get approximately the same answer; the triceps are characteristic of all.

In examining the triceps, the fulcrum *(F)* is the center of action in the shoulder joint. The top anchorage of the

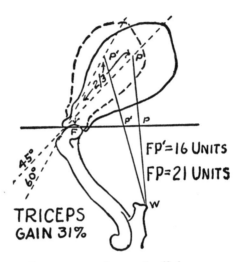

FP'=16 UNITS

FP=21 UNITS

TRICEPS GAIN 31%

Leverage action and efficiency are improved for every attached muscle on the 45-degree blade as compared with the 60. The triceps, from blade to elbow, illustrate this by the distance P is removed from F.

tricep is approximately two-thirds up the center line of the blade from the joint; so, a line drawn from this point *(P)* to the head of the radius in the forearm *(W)* will establish its distance from *F* by the intersection of the horizontal. We can measure the distance prescribed by the two blades and determine their value insofar as a mechanical advantage from leverage is concerned. In doing this, we will find that the 45-degree blade is at least 30 per cent more efficient than the 60-degree one.

"They can't step beyond their shoulder blades," my grandfather often said about both horses and dogs.

"You can measure the reach of a dog's front legs by the angle of his shoulder," an eminent English judge once informed us.

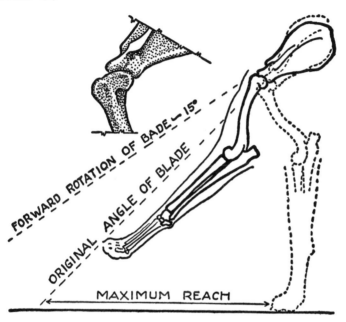

MAXIMUM REACH

The head of the Upper Arm has a knob that prevents the complete straightening of the Shoulder Joint and therefore limits the forward reach of the front leg. A line drawn down the center of the original blade position will mark the limit of the forward reach.

That is a feature of the shoulder blade which no breeder, interested in *well bent stifles, well angulated hindquarters, good drive* or any one of the various phrases by which back power is described, should overlook. You cannot put drive behind unless the front can take care of it without having a disorganized mechanism. The judge or owner, who admires or puts a dog up because of hindquarters without due consideration of this fact, is like the man who picks his wife "going away."

The shoulder blade has a socket with a nose thrust forward on it. The humerus has a bald head hooked to the top side with a knob that, as the joint is opened, strikes the nose of the shoulder blade socket and stops its movement in that direction. These are so located that the humerus will not open to a full 180 degrees but is checked between 140 and 165. This, with the 15-degree forward rotation of the blade, is still somewhat short of a complete reach. At the very best, the dog will not step beyond the point where a line drawn down through the center of the blade when stationary intersects the ground.

With the dog standing in natural stationary position, you can locate the center line of the blade by the ridge. Project this line to the ground and the pad will not extend beyond that in the stride. The question, insofar as it concerns conformation and the dog's smooth, progress in locomotion, is whether or not this puts the pad on the ground where momentum terminates.

PADDING AND POUNDING

The dog's gait, at whatever speed he is traveling, creates an arc, which might be likened to the trajectory of a bullet, and that is the first fiddle in the accompaniment.

The ideal point at which the pad should strike the ground is where momentum expends itself and the arc contacts the earth. Up to that point there are two forces active: momentum and gravity. When the forward reach is not sufficient to advance the pad to this point, dogs may meet the situation in one of four ways.

In one, the pad strikes the ground while both forces are active; that is, before the end of the arc has been reached. This slams the pad into the ground with a much harder, skidding action than should be necessary. The dog is "pounding" and the whole front assembly must absorb an increased shock.

Some dogs bring into play the abductor muscles of the forearm, those that bend the elbow. These lift the leg and pad higher, suspending them in the air for a fraction longer time and then drop the pad into place. Many breeders and ringside observers have admired this characteristic.

The reach should be sufficient to enable the pad to strike the ground at the point where the momentum arc does. Conformation of front with the back assembly which produces this arc is essential. The 45-degree blade, giving maximum reach, is the best answer for this problem.

"Watch that baby pick up those front feet," is not an unusual comment, "like a high stepping horse."

In carriage-horse days, this action was also admired by some in matched teams but it must be remembered that these horses covered very little ground and usually at a slow pace. It was not unusual in those days for Standard-bred trotters, too slow for the track, to be shod with a long toe and short heel and sometimes have their tendons "fired" and contracted to produce this high knee lift when sold as matched teams for buggy use.

This not only requires additional muscular effort but breaks the tautness of the leg, in which condition it should be at the time of striking the ground. For a time it will be brought back somewhat automatically into tension when it is allowed to straighten; but, as the dog grows tired, this may not be complete and the dog will stumble.

A third means of meeting this condition is through the action of the rearing muscles. These take on the burden of suspending the forequarters by producing a little more "lift" than they normally would be required to do. You

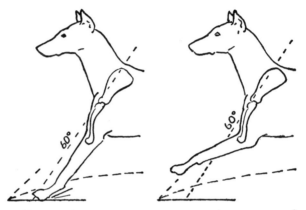

Two major faults in front leg action are pounding and padding. The front leg in the first sketch is hitting the ground before momentum has expended itself, falling short of the arc, and is pounding or suffering unnecessary shock. The second dog, to avoid this, is padding by breaking the tension of his leg and lifting it higher but as he tires he will eventually fail to bring it back into tension before striking the ground and come a cropper. These faults will fall to the 60-degree blade when the back drive is too strong for it.

see this more often in the gallop than other gaits. The dog will not have a level gallop but will resemble a rocking horse bobbing across the field. Needless to say, these dogs lack both speed and endurance for they use energy going up as well as going away.

If the dog was consistently running down hill, the 60-degree blade might be as effective as is the 45 on level ground, due to the delayed impact. Unfortunately, life is not lived coasting down grade.

The most fortunate dog, having to solve this problem, is the one that cuts down his back drive, even though he may have excellent power there, until it matches his front. Unless one realizes what he is doing, the animal might be criticized as: "He's got plenty of angulation in those back legs but he will not step out—short gaited." We certainly would not class the dog as perfect, but we do give him more credit for not slamming it into his front legs than if he utilized his push to the fullest extent.

Slow-moving, heavy draft animals might do with a blade lacking in maximum layback. Oxen have blades approaching the vertical and, weight for weight, can out-pull horses in slow motion and over bad footing. This may account for the fact that in some breeds we ask for *slightly sloping* or *moderately sloping shoulders*. Among these are the Alaskan Malamute, Mastiff, Bullmastiff, Chow, and Dalmatian. However, the majority of dogs should be better equipped for movement than oxen.

The lay-back of the shoulder blade in your dog can be determined by first posing him so that the blade is in natural position and then observing the angle which the ridge takes as compared to the ground.

Locate the approximate center of the blade and pose the front leg so that the heel pad is under this center. This position gives you the natural position of the blade when in static balance or when the dog is carrying the weight of the forehand with all opposing forces nearly equalized. The terrier front assumes this position when the pad is a little advanced of the vertical center of gravity; perhaps with the elbow under it, depending on the shortness of the upper arm.

A PROBLEM IN POSING

If you pose the dog with a normal front, as is often done in the show ring, by lifting the front so that the legs are extended and then dropping the dog so that the pads are advanced of the vertical center giving a straighter line to the front profile you will increase the lay-back to the blade from its true position. This is due to the fact that the blade rotates on its center and that the humerus or upper arm is brought forward pushing the shoulder joint upward

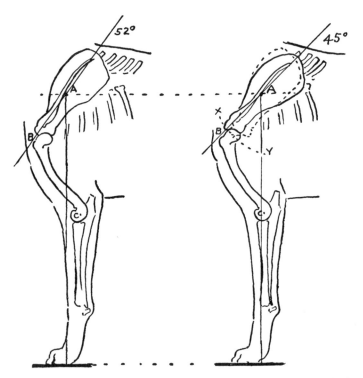

The true angulation or lay-back of the shoulder blade is revealed only when the heel-pad stands directly under the center (A) of the blade. The blade pivots on its center A, the radius A-B remains the same, the length of the upper arm B-C remains the same; therefore when C is brought forward, by moving the pad, the point B is thrust upward along the arc X-Y which is prescribed by the radius A-B. This rotates the blade and gives a false impression of its angulation. As illustrated, a 52-degree lay-back can be made to appear as a 45-degree lay-back.

which will in turn rotate the blade top to the rear. By this method you make say a 52-degree blade appear as a 45-degree blade; so, if you are looking for the correct answer, pose the dog with the heel pad under the center.

There is a decided ridge running from joint to upper tip of the blade which follows an approximate center line and which can easily be located by the finger tips; judge this in its relation to the ground.

Not infrequently, we have been challenged for an "authority" when stating that the shoulder blade should lie back 45 degrees, the breeder or judge feeling that unless some writer within his realm had made the specific statement it did not apply to his breed.

At least 12 popular breeds ask for shoulders *long and sloping* with some adding *well into the back*. Twenty-five want shoulders *sloping* or *oblique*. A few say, *well sloped backwards*. Some standards make no comment at all about the set of the blade, the Irish Setter being one of these.

As pointed out previously, these terms came from the paddock and, to the man in the saddle, were synonymous with that found on a good horse which always approached 45 degrees. Therefore we are not amiss when we assume that the authors of those old standards had this angle in mind when they wrote in such terms.

The words "sloping" and "oblique" are described in the dictionary as applying to any deviation from the horizontal or perpendicular. If we take them literally, an 85-degree blade would fit many standards. We doubt if any show-ring judge would pass such a shoulder even though it did comply literally with the standard, solely because he knows that is not an efficient position. That brings us to the question of efficient position—the most efficient, to be precise. Any close study of the blade for utility and service will take you straight to the 45-degree blade.

Summarizing it, we find the largest possible blade on

the given dog, the longest and widest muscles, the greatest arc of action in movement, improved lift of gravity and by its very size and angle forced to lie on the side of the thoracic frame and apply its movement parallel to the line of locomotion.

Regardless of whether the feature is treated lightly or described by enigmatic phrases all laws of dynamics, whether static or kinetic, as well as the study of gaits afield bear out the fact that the most adequate for the position of a shoulder blade is on the 45-degree angle. In all breeds the foundation of the front assembly is the shoulder blade and this should be the soundest which it is possible to procure.

11

Balanced Fronts

THE vaudeville performer balancing spinning plates atop long poles, which rest on chin or forehead, and a cantilever or suspension bridge may seem a far cry from the front assembly of a dog; even so the dog might be termed "brother to a bridge." His front assembly must be dynamically balanced for it to function with the highest degree of efficiency even as the bridge and jugler's tricks.

Dynamics is the science which investigates the action of force. It is divided into *statics,* dealing with forces at rest, and *kinetics,* dealing with forces in motion. Such statements are merely words—a scrap of paper from a philologist for Jurgen to wave in the wind—unless we make and understand a practical application of them to the animal in question.

The front of a sound horse is in static balance which permits him to rest while standing on all fours. The lack of such balance puts the quiver in the Fox Terrier's pastern. We can look to the winner of the Preakness or to one of the big-time bird dog field trials for examples in kinetic balance, and to those sporting dogs which because of its lack roll over the fields like rocking horses.

Static balance can be illustrated by the showman who balances a steel ball on the tip of a flexible foil. The tip of the foil and the heel of its hilt must remain directly under the center of gravity of the ball. Let either one deviate from this line and the showman's act is over.

STATIC BALANCE

We can plot two fronts which are in static balance and which are applicable to the majority of our dogs. Starting first with a 45-degree blade, a vertical line from the ground passing through the center point of suspension of the blade indicates the vertical center of gravity. The inter-

Static or stationary balance is illustrated by this showman whose foil can bend from here to yonder so long as the hilt remains under the center of gravity of the whole.

section point will be approximately the same on a more upright blade; that is, on the center of the blade itself, the pivot of the blade, for the muscular suspension indicates that.

The vertical line of support, then, must have its base centered on this line even as the heel of the foil must come directly under the center of gravity in the ball. The heel pad is the logical and most efficient part of the pad for supporting weight; therefore, this should be placed on the intersection of the vertical line with the ground. The remainder of the bones which make up the support can follow whatever pattern is more suitable for the mission of the individual dog.

It matters not what course the support takes from the center of gravity in an object to the base of its support. The foil can bend as much as it chooses or go into contortions so long as the hilt is directly under the center of gravity. That is a law of mechanics we should bear in mind as we make a study of any individual dog's legs and supports.

That being true, the columnar support can come down precisely on the vertical line, as the pole would under the juggler's spinning plate, or back behind the line reaching its base by a bent pastern into the line. We have both types represented among our dogs. However, the latter is far more satisfactory even if only in a slightly modified state. A good field trial Pointer, or a horse illustrates the modified state; the German Shepherd is an example of the more extreme.

In either of these fronts, if the pad is not under the center of gravity, the pastern and pad will take a beating wherever the dog stands, strides or steps. If the pad is behind the line, the pastern being too straight to set it under, the weight will be carried on the toes or digits rather than on the heel of the pad. The foot may break down and flatten out or the pastern go down below the angle at which its natural structure intended. In case the pad is in front of this line, the heel has a tendency to roll backward, putting weight on the sesamoid bone, at the same time throwing the navicular bone out.

Any horseman who has spent much time around the track can tell you about navicular and sesamoid trouble, for those two little bones break down many a horse, pri-

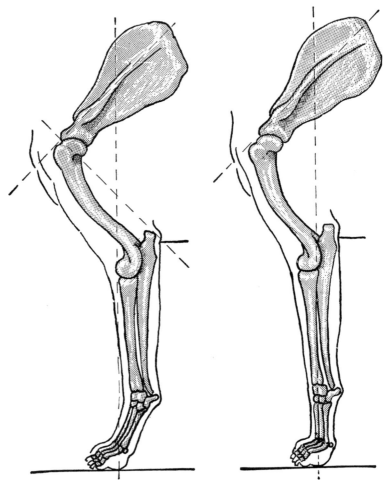

The center of gravity in the front assembly passes upward through the center of the shoulder blade. For static balance, the heel of the pad must be placed directly on this vertical line. If the heel is behind this, the weight is carried on the toes. If in front of it, there is always an extra muscular strain or leverage applied in sustaining weight because the assembly is out of static balance.

marily because the individual is not in dynamic balance in the front assembly. Animals in which the columnar support comes down in front of vertical line are definitely out of static balance. This type of front, which is found is some terriers, will be discussed at length as a special front.

POWER DERIVED FROM EXTENSION

The power derived from the front leg and its ability to absorb shock are in direct ratio to the difference between its extended and contracted length. Therefore the length of the humerus or upper arm has a specific bearing on this. In fact, anything that gives greater length without increasing natural height steps up this ratio.

Humerus length can be increased three ways: 1) reduce the size of the blade; 2) drop the elbow below the brisket; 3) set it at 90 degrees to the blade and let it extend further back on the body.

Reducing the shoulder blade will produce a greater loss than could possibly be gained for the humerus. This blade is now smaller on all dogs in proportion to the body than that found on a good front in horses. If any change is to be sought in this, it should be to enlarge it and derive greater muscular support.

Dropping the elbow below the brisket will be accomplished as a rule by shortening the bones of the forearm which in turn shortens their muscles and reduces their efficiency and that of the pads, for the tendons of these muscles activate the digits. Where this has been done, the humerus has had a tendency to assume an almost vertical set and bring the columnar support in advance of the center of gravity, putting the front out of static balance. This is seen on some gazehounds despite the fact that a few of these standards specifically request that the forearm be kept relatively long.

Setting the humerus as nearly as possible to a 90-degree

angle from the blade is the most efficient means of increasing its length. Several standards ask for a set of this type, some for the humerus to be as long as the blade. When this is done the blade and humerus form a right-angle triangle with two equal sides. It puts the columnar sup-

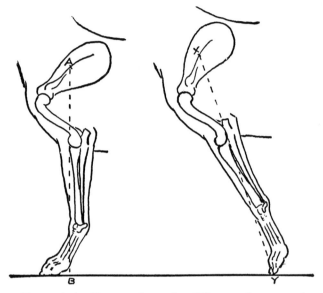

Power is in direct ratio to the difference between the contracted and extended length of the leg, that is, between X-Y and A-B as shown in the sketch. The leg assumed the maximum contraction as the center of gravity in the shoulder passes over the heel pad. Maximum length is accomplished just before the pad leaves the ground. In this sketch the ratio is that of 37½ units to 42.

port back of the vertical center of gravity and requires a bent pastern to keep the assembly in static balance. A well developed front of this type is greatly responsible for the sweeping gait seen on so many German Shepherds.

The long humerus has several distinct advantages. It increases the length of such muscles as the triceps and those activating the forearm. Its elongation is a specific gain in the functional length of the leg, increasing its adsorption, power generation, and ability to lift the center of gravity. The long upper arm will have a much greater arc of travel, being particularly advantageous to the follow-through, an action appreciated by golfers and baseball players but seldom considered by dog breeders with respect to leg action.

One of the best fronts on domestic animals is that of the Thoroughbred and Standardbred horses. This fact has been well established by racers and hunters as well as by the cavalry and artillery. While the horse breaks down more often in front, showing that to be his weakest point, his front assembly is put together more efficiently than that of most domestic animals. This is due to his shoulder and upper arm units, his weakness coming below those bones. The upper arm and shoulder blade of the horse could well be the ideal for the majority of our dogs' working and living conditions. Below these two bones we could stick to what we have in good working dogs and would then improve on both assemblies.

EFFICIENT PASTERNS

Horsemen have long asked for "knees well let down or close to the ground" in an effort to improve the mechanical advantage of that joint, which is the same as the pastern in the dog. The dog has the advantage of the joint well let down and close to the ground. It is also much better arranged internally due to a more efficient shape to the pisiform for application of leverage.

Some breeders advocate a straight-set pastern and we find some breeds with it. It functions as a straight joint on the horse, we are told, and therefore it should on the dog. That question can be answered in a few words but it will take some analysis to substantiate the answer. First we might compare the manner in which the two assemblies make use of this joint and apply force through it. They do not work alike. Refer to illustration on page 107.

The horse, as you will note, stands and lands in movement on the first digit. His second and third digits slope up from this and by their flexible arrangement absorb the shock of concussion when the hoof lands. These give down until they almost touch the ground at high speed, then when the muscles straighten them up power is applied. The force of the action is transmitted into the large metacarpal, five bones fused into one, to reach the horse's knee in a straight line.

The dog's foot strikes the ground on his heel pad and the shock of that concussion does not pass through the digits but goes directly into the metacarpals. These, then, must be so arranged that they can cushion the shock as did the second and third digits for the horse. The only practical arrangement is that they be inclined as are the horse's digits. This means that the pastern must bend and not stand rigid.

As the metacarpals in the dog's leg are much shorter proportionately than their fusion in the horse's leg their leverage action is more efficient as regards muscular strength, therefore the joint is able to function flexibly. It is because of the severe leverage that the horse's knee cannot function flexibly in receiving shock, and horsemen criticise the *calf-knee,* one that bends backward. A calf-kneed horse is more sure footed on rough ground, though.

Next, we might consider the function of the joint when set straight. We know that it can bend both forward and backward. Any double hinged joint set on dead center will bear weight efficiently as long as its position is not disturbed. If it is moved slightly out of line, then the two opposing forces which control it must be equal in strength or one will eventually suffer. If it is slightly off-center in natural position one force can be dominant. It

is much easier to control one dominant force than maintain equality in forces.

The front members of the bones that make up the pastern are all bearing bones with no provision for leverage.
The muscles coming down the front part of the leg con-

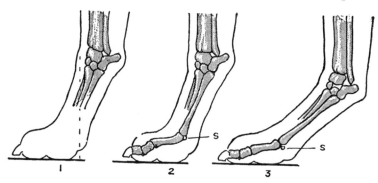

Well bent pasterns follow two patterns. 1) The bend is
above the bone assembly, between it and the forearm. 2) The
bend is below the bone assembly, between it and the metacarpals, the face of the assembly remaining in line with the forearm.
Of the two, the former is usually encountered and is preferable.
3) This sketch shows a broken-down pastern, either inherited or
physically weak. Note the displaced bones in the assembly, the
bearing of weight by the pisiform at an unnatural and inefficient angle. Note also that the sesamoid (S) bone is out of position, which will cause as much trouble as the disarranged
pastern joint. This condition usually flattens out the foot. The
weight is not carried by the column of bones but by the muscles
and tendons coming down the back side of the leg.

tinue on to the metacarpals and digits: these muscles are
not relatively powerful, for their major work is to swing
the pad forward without any load on it. Yet these muscles are supposed to prevent *knuckling over* in a straight
pastern.

Muscles on the back side of the leg do attach themselves
to the pastern assembly and apply leverage to the pisiform. This bone also has a counterbalancing muscle attached to it and to the fifth metacarpal which likely does

the majority of the work in maintaining a straight set to the joint. These muscles are strong enough to stand the concussion received in movement and are therefore capable of maintaining weight and controlling the joint to better advantage than those forward. This physical construction is not in balance as regards power application fore and aft so we court trouble by asking it to stay in balance even for that period in which the dog remains stationary.

Place the knuckles of your hand on the table top and press straight down on them. Hold the wrist joint, which is the same as the dog's pastern, so that it forms a vertical line. In this position it does bear weight without effort. Now move it slightly forward out of line and notice the quiver that comes into it, which is what happens when you see the quivering pasterns, the knuckling over of many terriers in the ring and in older dogs which had straight pasterns.

THE BROKEN-DOWN PASTERN

Sloping pasterns are not to be confused with broken-down pasterns. The slope should not start in the joint itself but either above it or below it, keeping this group of bones in compact harmony. Sometimes we get angulation from both points which can be approved so long as the carpal assembly remains intact. If it starts above the pastern joint, then the angulation comes from the base of the radius and the length of the ulna. When it is below the joint, the metacarpals run straight but assume more curve right at their heads and the one on which the pisiform sits is relatively longer than the others.

The broken-down pastern finds the carpal assembly awry and askew and not supporting the weight carried by the leg but putting this burden on the muscles whose tendons act over the pisiform and down to contract the digits.

Two mechanical advantages may accrue from a straight-set pastern: a straight column of bones will bear more weight for the work is then taken off the muscles, and long metacarpals cannot apply as much leverage on operating muscles. The dog does not have to bear weight other than that of his own body and his metacarpals are relatively short, so these advantages are not important enough to off-set the disadvantages acquired by the straight pastern.

Too much bend would be just as undesirable, therefore we should locate the proper amount needed. The bend does three things: 1) prevents knuckling over and undue tax on muscles involved in that; 2) absorbs the shock of concussion; 3) and provides greater lift to the center of gravity by letting the bones below the pastern enter into that action. Any slight bend off-center will take care of the first while it requires a little more flexibility to be efficient in the other two.

The slope should always be sufficient to bring the heel of the pad under the center of gravity. A large blade and long upper arm, set at 90 degrees, will require consider-able slope for this. If the assembly puts the pad in front of the vertical center, then the pastern should slope enough to get it off direct center and to give it flexibility.

CAT-FOOT AND HARE-FOOT

The relative merits of the two types of feet recognized on dogs depend entirely on the purpose to which they are being put. We have encountered considerable miscon-ception as to what constitutes a cat-foot and hare-foot. Actually there is only one difference, the length of the third digital bone. In the hare-foot, the third digital bone, the one parallel to the ground, is longer than the same bone in the cat-foot. As the length of one bone tends to influence that of another, the second and third digits in the hare-foot may be relatively longer but the foot should lose none of its compactness. Under no circumstances should a broken-down cat-foot be mistaken for a hare-foot.

The long third digit increases leverage action and therefore speed. The inverse, found in the cat-foot, improves endurance. The weight to be lifted comes down the meta-

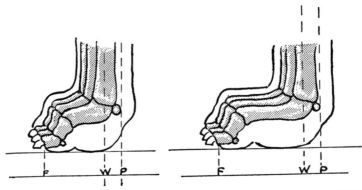

The Cat-foot, as shown in the first sketch, has a short third digital bone, which shortens the distance between F and P and requires less power to lift W, therefore it is less fatiguing. The Hare-foot, shown in the second sketch, has a long third digital bone which makes for a longer leverage and more speed but is more fatiguing. Both of these feet should be compact with the second digital bone standing between 45 and 60 degrees to the ground line, the nearer the perpendicular, the better.

carpals, the power applied is through the tendons back of these and the fulcrum or fixed point is the toe contact with the ground. In the hare-foot we lengthen *F-W* and *F-P* without changing the relation of *W-P* which produces more action with a given power but likewise increases the load and hastens fatigue. The cat-foot takes us in the other direction.

In working rough ground, working continuously or just knocking about the house, the cat-foot is the more logical answer. It is less subject to injury and does not require as much muscular effort. Either one though must be compact, stand well up on the first digit and have thick heel pads.

Over the years, we have known but one good running Whippet—there may have been more—that had a cat-foot. This Whippet was a cross with a Bull Terrier, bred by Felix Leser and Willie Kelley. During the twenties, we came in contact with hundreds of top-running Greyhounds on the plains of the West and the tracks of Butte, St. Louis, Shrevesport and New Orleans without recalling a single cat-foot; this despite the fact that their standard seeks a compromise.

The majority of fast-running Foxhounds, particularly those run at night on wolves, bobcats and fox, usually have a hare-foot. The American Foxhound wants a fox-like foot, which is relatively the same. The Englishman, usually well informed as to what makes a good dog, writes in the standard for the English Foxhound asking for *"legs as straight as a post"* and *"feet . . . round and cat-like."* Then continues in this same standard with: *"The desire for straightness is carried to excess, as the very straight leg soon knuckles over, and this defect may almost always be seen more or less in old stallion hounds."*

Conservation of energy and relative freedom from injuries make it advisable to seek the cat-foot on the majority of working and pet dogs. The shorter, more compact foot is less subject to injuries and its reduced leverage action lessens the strain on the ligaments. It is, we believe, easier to acquire a good cat-foot in breeding than a good hare-foot.

PADS AND DEW CLAWS

The conditions of the pads or soles are important to a good foot. If the heel pad is thick and well built up it will not only stand more shock and rough use over the ground but will increase endurance by shortening the leverage action. Paper feet should never be tolerated, neither should splay feet; forgive any of the other faults that might accrue in them in preference to either of these. Few things are any more important to a dog in the home or afield than good feet.

The dew claw is the termination of the fifth metacarpal

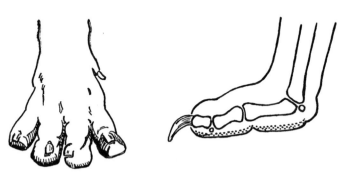

SPLAY FEET, as shown in first sketch, have the toes spread, often with daylight between them; they lack compactness and strength and are more subject to injury afield. PAPER FEET, as shown in the second sketch, have thin soles or pads. Because the heel pad is thin and is not elevating the third digital bone, the whole foot usually breaks down. DEW CLAWS, the fifth toe as shown in the first sketch, are called for by some standards and usually appear on the front legs if not the back. They are subject to injury afield and are removed from newborn pups by many breeders.

in the front leg and metatarsal in the back leg. This is comparable to the thumb and big toe in man but has come to serve no real purpose for the dog. Some standards demand them both front and back and probably have discovered some specific reason for this requirement.

Generally they are removed from the leg before the pup opens its eyes for then they can be clipped away quite easily. The practice of removing them is more often directed toward the back leg, leaving them on the front. In some breeds they do not show up at all or only occasionally, particularly on the back legs. Dogs that work afield over rough or frozen ground should have them removed lest they strike sharp edges and become torn or injured. Removal also adds a certain neatness to the line of the leg that otherwise is lacking.

Recently we encountered a handler at an Eastern show with a St. Bernard which had the best legs and feet we had seen on one in many years. "The judge put him down," the handler said, "and I'm going back after the judging to ask why." That we wanted to hear and trailed along.

"I'm glad you came back," the judge said, "I want to show you something." Then he turned and requested the owner of the winning dog to bring the dog in the ring. He did; and the judge took hold of the dog's head and opened his eyes. "Did you ever see such dark eyes—they're the best in the country."

"Does that compensate for him being cow-hocked and so splay footed that his toes hardly know which direction he's going?"

"Ah, he's just two years old—give him time and he'll come up on those feet and those hocks'll straighten out."

"Mister, I got a two-year-old heifer in my pasture, do you mean that in time she's not going to be cow-hocked?"

The incident reminded us of a 50-dollar saddle on a 20-dollar horse. Sometimes roadwork and restoration of good health will tighten a dog's foot but generally a bad foot will only get worse with age and, as this has to support the entire dog when he is moving or standing still, it should always be one of major considerations for big ones or little ones alike.

12

Special Fronts

YEARS ago an itinerant tinker strolled into a rural Scottish merchant's place, tossed his pots and pans on the counter and began dickering with the merchant on the sale price of an armful of pelts. The merchant examined them, and they finally reached a unit agreement.

"There are twelve," the tinker said as he multiplied the total out on a scrap of paper.

The merchant counted them and then exclaimed, "There are only eleven!"

"Aye, but I left my Sandy in a hole down the road—he'll be along in a few minutes with the other one."

Certainly those fellows were not worried about anything in their terriers except efficient delivery from the ground. Going to ground, however, for the dog presented problems that were not a part of surface work. The holes were not large and the rodent usually had a system of filling his hole up after him when being pursued. This meant that they could use only a small, normal dog, perhaps too small to cope with the rodent, or breed themselves bigger, more powerful dogs which could work their way into these holes and do a job after they got there.

These dogs usually had to work with their briskets on the ground. They had to have complete freedom of action of the upper arm or the digging stroke would be cut short almost before it began. That is, the elbow had to be set high enough to create an arc in action that did not reach below this brisket line or the leg's stroke would be locked where the elbow stopped.

STRAIGHT TERRIER FRONT

Breeders accomplished this free action of the front leg by two distinctly different methods. One, of which the Fox Terrier is an example, is characterized by a *straight front*. The other, of which the Scottie and Dachshund are types, sets the dog's body down between a reduced or

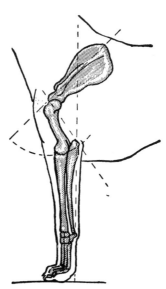

THE TERRIER FRONT gets its appearance of straightness of face line by shortening the Upper Arm so that the arc of elbow travel is above the brisket line. The blade should not be reduced in size or be set upright, and there should be a slight bend to pasterns though few have it. This front is never in static or kinetic balance.

miniature shoulder assembly. Both styles have back legs to correspond.

These methods each accomplished the end desired even though they had to make certain sacrifices in other features to get it. The changes and sacrifices are counter to the natural tendencies of the dog's basic heritage, which is apt to be persistent in upsetting the game at any time unless the rules are understood and closely watched. Faults come like ghosts in the night to materialize by day into unwanted permanent guests, often refusing to leave until you burn the house and make a new start.

The straight front, such as the terriers with a high center

of gravity have, was developed by retaining a shoulder blade of normal comparative size and then shortening the humerus or upper arm sufficiently for its arc of action to remain above the brisket line. The humerus assumed a more or less vertical position, atop straight legs and pasterns which give the impression of a straight front.

The idea of the foundation, if it can be maintained, is sound, for all that has been said about the value of a 45-degree layback to the blade applies here. Many of the standards for these dogs go to specific details in trying to impress the desirability of a blade that at least approaches this position. The leg action in this arrangement is kept well in advance of the brisket and shoulder point when the dog is digging.

There are mechanical advantages other than free elbow action which accrue to this short upper arm. It is drawn back by the great dorsal and pectoral muscles with attachments (P) near the shoulder joint (F) and a reduced distance from there to the elbow (W), so that the function of WPF is to a mechanical advantage, delivering power to move a greater weight without the normal cost in energy per pound.

The leverage action on the forearm at the elbow by the triceps is not affected. This could be increased to an advantage by the lengthening of the ulna extension or a greater outward curve of its tip. We find such an ulna crown highly developed in mountain sheep and many other animals. Though it would aid any dog, it could be a decided advantage to the one that digs.

By retaining a length of forearm comparable with what a dog of that size would naturally have, breeders have not shortened the muscles which activate the pastern and foot when the dog is digging; that is, those which bend the pastern backward and draw the pad with it.

In getting a front of this type, apparently breeders had but one change to make in the dog, that of shortening the humerus. This seemed to simplify the task and probably did for a while; but the very singleness of it made it complex because of nature's laws.

One of the ghosts continually stalking this front is a part of the compound which refuses to be simplified—the natural tendency for anything, affecting one bone in an assembly, to cast its influence on the nearest and closest related bone. So, instead of working one by one, it wants to go two by two and comes up with a small, inefficient shoulder blade.

These shoulder blades have a tendency not only to shorten and get smaller but to assume a more vertical angle. You will find any number of them set in this manner and falling quite short of reaching up to the withers point. We have found Fox Terriers in the ring with as much as an inch between top of blade and the withers crown, which indicates to what extent it can go in comparison to the dog. Unfortunately such a set tends to give the dog the appearance of a "straighter front" and please the eye of a novice and some judges.

Such a blade defeats the originators' idea of maintaining a good foundation for the front. Its tendency to go small is likely due to the influence of the small humerus, but its vertical set, bringing the center of gravity forward, is probably nature's effort to put the front back in dynamic balance. There is no practical means of measuring the cause and effect but there is visual evidence of the latter.

Straight pasterns are an habitual accompaniment to this front even if those who wrote the standards had not dictated them, for there is always a pronounced tendency to retain balance whether we want it or not. Bent pasterns under a fore limb so far in advance of the vertical center would only put the pads that much more advanced. By designating them to begin with, breeders helped to pull the humerus into a vertical position and slap a straight line from shoulder point to pad.

KNUCKLING OVER

These straight pasterns brought with them all the troubles that they can muster; the most dominant being *knuckling over* and *quivering*. Frankly, there can be no more serious fault in any front than these two and the influence they have on the pad.

One needs only to watch the straight-pasterned dogs in a show ring to realize how prevalent these characteristics have become. In an entry of 30-odd of one popular breed at a recent show, we counted 19 that knuckled over or quivered, and these dogs were relatively young and supposedly in sound show condition. Three of them were owned by enthusiastic breeders who also had good horses, and we wondered how they would react had we tried to sell them a horse with jittery knees.

There is only one logical correction for this condition—give the pastern enough bend to take the joint off dead center and keep it there. True, this takes the front still more out of balance but it never will be in balance so there is no quibble on that point. This would be more effective in digging and better suited to absorbing shock and taking weight off the toes. Throwing weight on the toes soon flattens them out and breaks down the arches.

The pastern, which has gone down from weakness and strain put on it, is not to be confused with one which has an intended structural set off-center. When this pastern first went down, it was because of ligament weakness which soon reflects itself in flattened toes.

Another trouble this front encounters is lack of balance with the drive of the rear assembly which remained normal and gets an emphasis on angulation by standards and breeders. Many of the latter go to great length in trying to secure acute angulation in the back leg. While this is an advantage to the dog in making a kill, for it gives him more push, that same push makes a *padder* or a *pounder* out of him in movement. As long as his shoulder blades are *well laid back* his fore stride is relatively good.

This front accomplishes the end which the original breeders had in mind, so long as a sound foundation is maintained and too much stress is not put on the straightness of the pastern. Only a small percentage of these dogs are sent to ground but those which are good workers and good movers certainly get about their kennels and homes with greater ease.

LOW CENTER OF GRAVITY FRONTS

We referred to the second means of getting elbow action above brisket line with the word "miniature" but this, although classifying, is not truly descriptive. This front reduces both length of upper and forearm as well as the blade so that the unit can be set high enough on the dog's body to keep the elbow action above the desired line. The bones themselves are kept as massive as possible and often have as much cross-section as they would had the dogs followed the natural pattern for their size.

The Dachshund's pad is likely as large as if the dog had normal daylight beneath him. The same may be said of the Scottie and the Sealyham. It is primarily that the bone length has been reduced and this is rather proportionate from top of blade to the intersection with the pad. This reduction was as easy to accomplish as had breeders chosen to shorten one bone because of associate influence.

While this front does lose some of the advantages of leverage due to the short bones, it can remain in static and kinetic balance, a factor which contributes to endurance and smooth operation. It conforms rather well with extreme rear angulation for it has mechanical ability to relift the center of gravity and absorb shock. The laidback blade, angulated upper arm, and bent pastern all contribute to flexibility.

These dogs are usually "big dogs" that appear to be "little dogs" because of being low-set. Their bodies provide both large and long great dorsi and pectoral muscles that draw the upper arm back when the dog is digging. A short upper arm here again works to a leverage advantage for these muscles as regards fatigue.

Large, or more precisely, barrel bodies are responsible

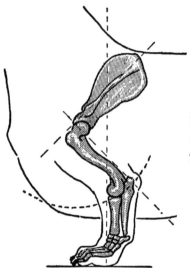

THE LOW CENTER OF GRAVITY FRONT, as seen on Dachshunds, Scotties and others, finds the whole assembly reduced in bone length and set high on the body so that elbow action is above brisket line. This front can be and often is in static and kinetic balance.

for one of the most persistent faults we find in dogs with this assembly. The majority of these dogs have been bred with round or oval ribs and, as they are let down between the small front assembly, give a greater pitch to the blade than would be the case with a larger blade. That is, the blade is set high on the arc and is inclined outward from the withers to the shoulder point which may fall at the widest part of the dog's body.

This position makes it impossible for the assembly to be in balance when viewed from the front unless the pads are placed under the body so that they come beneath the

center of the blade, which often results in a curved forearm. The greatest danger in this position though is the
blade's persistence to slide forward on the rib structure
and give us two very undesirable conditions.

The blade is inclined to set more vertical (from side
view) than it should and, being on the front of the tho-

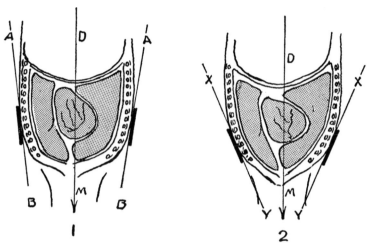

IN SPECIAL FRONTS the tendency of the blade-set is to
be in front of rather than beside the dog's rib structure. 1) The
blade set is but slightly forward. 2) It is well forward, creeping
toward the neck. Leg action is along lines A-B and X-Y and
in neither case is parallel to that of movement M-D. Inefficiency
increases with the degree of deviation from M-D.

racic section instead of on the side, assumes a bias to the
spinal column, the line of its normal action, and that of
body travel. The point of the blade when acting either
describes an arc around the rib structure, or a line which
plots the hypotenuse of a right-angled triangle rather than
one which would be parallel to the line of progress. It
therefore has an action loss equal to the difference between the hypotenuse and the fore and aft side of the
triangle.

The whole assembly, when the blade is forward, is

based more on the neck ligament than the thoracic section, and that poor ligament has enough to do without saddling it with extra work.

Success afield has tested this front and found that it gives a practical answer to the requirements of going-to-ground. It will so long as the shoulder blade is placed right and the assembly is kept in dynamic balance.

The Bulldog furnishes another example of a big dog taken down to the ground with shortened bones in the leg assemblies. This was not for the same reason as the Scottie and other terriers but to give him a low center of gravity and make it more difficult to upset him. He is hard to upset.

Several years ago at Cochrane, Ontario, we saw a fight between one of these fellows and a Husky on which something like a thousand dollars had been bet. The Husky, a slasher, kept charging in and out. The Bulldog kept moving in, but failed to gain a single point during the first 20 minutes. Then the Husky, which could almost walk over squatty without brushing the hairs on his belly, ended one if his charges with a characteristic shoulder buck. Instead of bouncing the Bulldog, he went right on over him as though he had hit a tree stump and rolled over twice before getting on his feet.

Later he must have forgotten this experience for he tried another shoulder buck but, being tired, was not quite as quick to regain his feet. Squatty got him this time and that ended the fight. On neither of the bucks did the Bulldog seem to give an inch though a 90-pound Husky can put a lot of power in his rush.

The major difference between the Bulldog front and any of the other low-set dogs shows up only when viewing the dog from the front and not the side. This is an effort to keep the body support vertical under the four corners of the rectangle at all times with the idea that the dog is more difficult to upset from that support. This is a feature that we will discuss further when considering kinetic balance coming and going.

The Bulldog's front falls heir to all the faults that accrue to the low center of gravity and the body let down between the assemblies, the most prevalent one being shoulder blades in front of and not along the side of the thoric structure with its action on the bias.

THE RACING FRONT

The racing front as seen on Whippets, Greyhounds and other double suspension travelers, in fact all gazehounds,

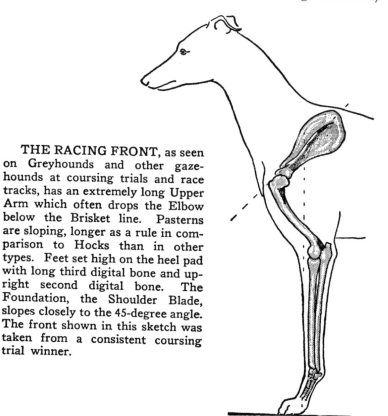

THE RACING FRONT, as seen on Greyhounds and other gazehounds at coursing trials and race tracks, has an extremely long Upper Arm which often drops the Elbow below the Brisket line. Pasterns are sloping, longer as a rule in comparison to Hocks than in other types. Feet set high on the heel pad with long third digital bone and upright second digital bone. The Foundation, the Shoulder Blade, slopes closely to the 45-degree angle. The front shown in this sketch was taken from a consistent coursing trial winner.

falls into the special class as it is the only front required to produce suspension. We do not ask normal fronts to add power to locomotion to any high degree, driving power being almost overlooked in their consideration. This is true of horses as well as dogs. But the racing front must produce driving power in addition to doing all the other offices of that assembly.

This front was developed several hundreds of years ago, so far back in fact that we cannot be certain when it did start. Perhaps it is as old as the Greyhound type though it likely came into being quite later as breeders improved the type. Among the ancients of Arabia and Persia were some top-notch breeders of both horses and dogs, yet they reached a point in both of these and then stopped. Neither the Arabian horse nor the front of our gazehounds has been improved in the last few centuries.

The best fronts found on any of the gazehounds—Afghan, Saluki, Whippet, Borzoi—are likely those on the Greyhounds winning on the tracks and at coursing trials. The Greyhound as a variety comes in several types which vary but slightly. These are the Rampur, Kangaroo, Baleric, Phu-Quoc, Arabian and our own version developed in England and this country. Perhaps improved is more correct than developed.

This front starts with a shoulder blade laid back a good 50 to 45 degrees, usually the latter, and of such length as to extend half way down the dog's thoric structure. In length it compares with the depth of the body at the floating rib or the length of the head in front of the ears.

Below this blade is an upper arm or humerus equally as long and set at an angle which brings the elbow under the back edge of the top of the blade. This, an open angle approximating 130 degrees, drops the elbow below the brisket. Such a set makes the dog appear *straight in front*. Pasterns take on a slope of 10 to 15 degrees and usually bring the heel pad under the center of gravity and give the front a static balance.

This seems to be relatively what the various standards request:

Greyhound—*Shoulders placed as obliquely as possible, muscular without being loaded. Forelegs perfectly straight, set well into the shoulder . . . pasterns strong.*

Afghan Hound—*Shoulder, which should be long and sloping, and well laid back . . . forelegs, great length between elbow and ankle, elbows well tucked in; forefeet very large both in length and breadth, toes well arched . . . pasterns long and pads well down on the ground.* The latter forecasts a bent pastern, otherwise both the pastern and forearm could not be long.

Saluki—*Shoulders sloping and set well back . . . forelegs long from elbow to knee . . . feet, toes long and well arched.* The others follow closely this same idea.

The speed and push in this front comes from the long upper arm, sloping pasterns and hare-foot. The open angle between upper arm and blade lengthens the triceps and other muscles connecting the two and, as muscles contract two thirds their fleshy length, this increases action. The long forearm is not a particular advantage to speed except to provide long muscles flexing the toes.

ENDURANCE

For endurance we have always sought hocks and knees well let down or close to the ground. In other words, short pasterns on the dog and cannon-bones on the horse. In this case, though, we seek speed and extra push so we want a long pastern assembly. For this to be long, it must take a decided slope or the forearm be shortened, otherwise the dog will stand high in front which moves the center of gravity back in the body and defeats the purpose of the long head and neck. The slope cannot be such though as to throw the bones of the pastern joint out of weight-supporting line. This situation was discussed earlier when considering pasterns.

Feet are one of the most important parts of this front, for above everything else they must be good. The longer we can get the third digit the more leverage action can be put in the drive; with that, the second digit must set as nearly vertical as possible making the foot compact. The heel pad should be extremely thick and have plenty of cushion under it. This will absorb much of the shock of contact with the ground, take the weight-carrying strain off the first and second digits without breaking them down and flattening the feet, and improve the mechanical efficiency as regards leverage.

We said that this front had not been improved for quite a while. That referred to the general type. We do find more good fronts among a given number of dogs actually coursing and working than showed up several years ago. As to how it could be improved is a question which would require long and careful consideration. The cheetah and pronghorn antelope are much faster than any of our gazehounds. A part of this undoubtedly lies in their front assemblies, therefore we might take a pattern from them.

The pronghorn differs quite markedly from the gazehounds in general type, which somewhat puts it out of consideration. The cheetah, though, is not unlike them in general make-up and possibly could contribute highly to their improvement. They are approximately 5 per cent faster afoot and have about equal endurance.

13

Balance Coming and Going

THE noonday sun carved out the shadows as sharply as did the old native's knife the shavings from the white pine board and the young outlander shaded his eyes from its glare.

"Moon worshipper," he said and draped the word with a tinge of sarcasm.

"Moon worshipper?" the old man repeated without missing a slice of the white pine. "Iv no iddy what ye mean but I do know that the moon's a licking sight better'n the sun. It's cool 'n' nivver gits ye all drippin' . . . 'sides it shines when its dark 'n' man needs its light."

Often we have been reminded of that when listening to current arguments of dog fanciers and breeders. The old native had become so accustomed to the benefits of light that he had never given its source a second thought. He would willingly have traded the sun for the moon. He would have been astonished at the havoc he had wrought but he would not have realized that the resultant darkness and cold were due to his bad bargain.

"But the dog's legs must move parallel to each other . . ."

"Yes, and perpendicular to the ground . . ."

Those are ideas that have become ingrained in the minds of many fanciers. Whence they started, we do not know. Where they are going, we do know—trading the sun for the moon.

Perhaps they started by misconstruing the wording of some of the old standards. We might examine a few of these for this evidence:

173

The Fox Terrier—*The forelegs viewed from any direction must be straight with bone strong right down to the feet.*

The Great Dane—*. . . seen from the front and also from the side absolutely straight down to the pasterns.*

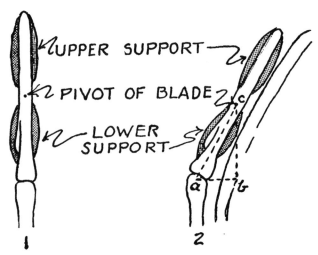

UPPER SUPPORT

PIVOT OF BLADE

LOWER SUPPORT

1   2

THE STATIC CENTER OF GRAVITY of the blade, viewed from the front, is between the upper and lower activating muscles or close to its center. The blade that sets upright (1) on the side of the dog's rib structure carries its load straight into the muscular assemblies. The blade angling inward (2) on the rib curve must counteract the leverage action set up by the angle as indicated in the triangle abc. Lengthening ab increases the force of leverage that must be overcome.

Pointer—*Front legs straight with no tendency to knuckle.*

Irish Terrier—*Legs . . . perfectly straight . . . both fore and hind legs should move straight forward when traveling.*

There are many others which call for *straight* legs and quite a number of writers have stressed that front legs should be straight from all sides, back legs straight when viewed from the rear, and all legs moving straight forward when traveling.

There is nothing in these statements though to indicate that the right and left front or rear legs should move parallel to one another or that they should show perpendicular to the ground when the dog is moving. The word "straight" was logically a reference to the bone, particularly that of the forearm or the forearm and pastern combined. It is understandable that this could be confused with being "perpendicular to the ground" as they would appear straighter then by optical illusion.

A Standardbred trotter, capable of going three to five 1-mile heats at close to record time in a single afternoon, must have sound legs and they are straight when viewed from all sides. Yet, when this horse draws up in front of the judge's stand, he will stop with his front hoofs almost touching one another. In this case the inward inclination is in a straight line from the shoulder joint to the ground but the leg is not perpendicular.

STATIC BALANCE IN FRONT

It is an effort to get static and kinetic balance that inclines these legs inward. The position of the shoulder blade prescribes the angle for static balance, and in a large number of breeds this is very slight. The speed at which the animal moves indicates the necessary angle for kinetic balance.

Considering the forward assembly strictly from a front view, we find that the curve of the ribs and the length of the blade will establish the angle at which the blade lies. With the well-rounded rib structure of the Bulldog we find a decided outward slant of the shoulder blade. The German Shepherd has ribs flat rather than barrel-shaped with shoulder blades set on flat against the body. Between these two, we have a variety of shoulder blade angles.

There is a static center of gravity to each of these blades when viewed from the front as well as from the side. For the assembly to be in static balance from this

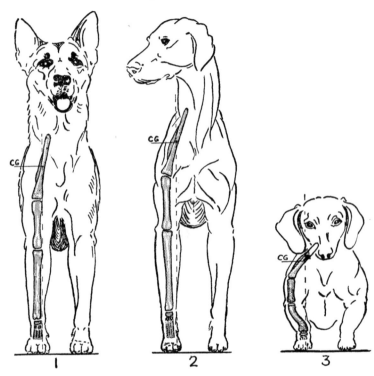

STATIC BALANCE from the front is accomplished by setting the heel, or at least the inner edge of it, under the vertical center of the shoulder blade. 1) The German Shepherd has an almost if not vertical set to the shoulder blade and therefore does not have to bring his feet in to get static balance. 2) The Pointer and many others have a slight and often decided slope of the blade so that they must set their feet well inside the vertical of the shoulder point to get balance. 3) The Dachshund with a decided slope to the blade will often have a curved forearm, setting his pasterns much closer together than the elbows and giving him static balance. Scotties and many others follow the same pattern.

position, the pad or base support should come directly
under this center, which is approximately in the center of
shoulder blade length due to muscular attachment and
support. Therefore, the dog with little or no outward

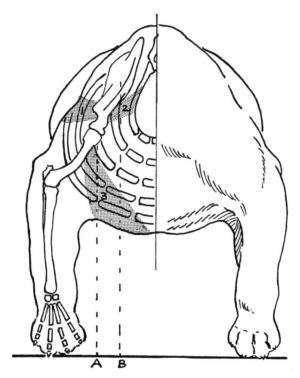

A B

In the Bulldog, by choice of breeders, there is
a decided attempt to prevent the natural tendency of the front leg to bow inward and bring
the assembly into static balance. The reason for
this is that they want a wide base of support
which fits in with the original purpose of the breed
although it is not used for bull baiting any more.
This wide base of support makes the dog more
difficult to upset. In the front shown, the pad
would have to come in to A for balance of blade
and upper arm and to B for complete static balance. As it sets there is extra leverage action on
muscles 1 and 2 (Serratus) and 3 (Pectoral).

inclination of the blade will not have to bring his pad inward very much to produce static balance. The dog with considerable inclination will have to bring the pad inward from the shoulder point to get it under the center of gravity.

Breeders of the very wide, low-set dogs have had to fight a battle against nature or accept a curve in the forearm as she insists on getting the pad into the balance line. Some standards recognize this fact and caution against it or make allowance for it as in the following:

Scottish Terrier—*Forelegs straight or slightly bent with elbows close to the body.*

Dachshund—*Joint between forearm and foot: These are closer together than the shoulder joints, so that the front does not appear absolutely straight.*

Bulldog—*Forelegs . . . straight . . . well developed calves, presenting a bowed outline . . . not to be curved or bandy, nor the feet brought too close together.*

Sealyham—*Forelegs . . . as straight as is consistent with chest being well let down between them.*

The last named breed classes "bowed legs" as a fault. There is in the wording of these a recognition of the tendency of the pads to get under the body. Also in nearly all these types the forearm is inclined to curve, yet it is possible to bring the pads under the dog with a straight forearm.

Dogs with a more vertical blade can often stand with legs almost parallel or perpendicular to the ground and maintain static balance.

SINGLE TRACKING

Kinetic or moving balance in the front assembly follows the same lines as static when viewed from the side, a fact which will be discussed later but which is not the

case when the assembly is seen coming toward you. Locomotive factors, of which lateral displacement is one,
mark a difference between the two balances from this
view.

If the dog had continual support at all four corners
such as is given by the wheels of a wagon, this change
would not be necessary. With the diagonal corners supporting, one after the other as in the trot, the dog can
converge these toward the center and get a continual support on one line like a bicycle. The fewer the number of
supports the body has, the more important it becomes
that this be done. In the walk, which has support on
three corners, converging toward a center line is not pronounced; but take away one of these supports, as in the
trot and pace, or two of them, as in the gallop, and you
have a different story. Speed means convergence for all.

Viewed from the front or rear, when the dog is stationary, the legs should set so that the pads are directly under
the center of muscular support of the shoulder blades. As
the dog starts to move, the positions are relatively the
same. From then on as the speed increases the pads converge to a single track beneath the actual center of the
dog. He begins with static balance and from there takes
off into the various positions of kinetic balance.

This is not just a theory but actual fact established
by every properly moving animal whether domestic or
wild. It is verified by mathematical calculations, all laws
of dynamics and relative physics and any conscientious
research you wish to apply to animals. The dogs which
have satisfied the judge or breeder and which do not
comply with this are but the exceptions that prove the
rule.

"The exception proves the rule" is a proverb that may
not always be understood. "Prove" originally meant to
try or *test,* derived from the Latin *probare* from which we

also get *probation.*   We have but to put these "exceptions" in the field to test the rule and find it as accurate
as the figures on the engineer's slide rule.

"But the dog will move too close," comes the habitual
protest from many.

One of the first lessons we learned about a horse was
worded by an old timer: "A horse can't move too close so
long as he does not interfere with himself."   The horseman meant "strike"; he was thinking of the trotter which

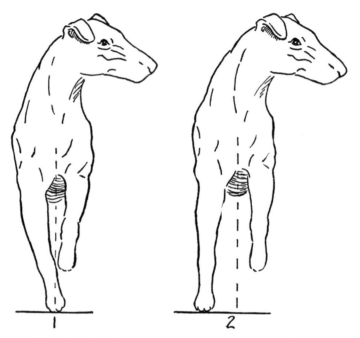

The Fox Terrier in sketch 1 is single tracking while
in sketch 2 the same dog is shown moving with legs perpendicular to the ground. In both cases front and back
legs are traveling in the same plane and moving straight
forward in compliance with the Standard. However, the
second position is out of kinetic balance, making no effort
to compensate or lessen lateral displacement and will not
stay afield with the single-tracking dog. The same applies to other breeds as well.

at high speed does "strike" and gives rise to the statement that a trotter is "no better than his boots."

The essence of the old man's statement is true, for the animal is not moving too close so long as his legs move true and do not interfere with one another.

Here we can refer back to such statements in standards as: *both fore and hind legs should move straight forward when traveling.* If the dog's pad, precisely on this center line or the one parallel to it which gives kinetic balance, is picked up and replaced on the same line at a more advanced station, it is certainly moving straight forward when traveling. It should not be picked up and swung in an arc to get it back on the line, for in that case it is not traveling straight forward but going through useless motion.

The front leg should operate with the column of bones from the shoulder joint to the pad as straight as the shape of the leg will permit. It should converge as near to the center line as the speed requires or the body width of the dog will allow. Wide, low-set dogs cannot be expected to single-track. The pad and leg should travel in a straight line parallel with that of travel, should not sweep around and in, nor work in a line angling away from this parallel even though the pad does come back to the line. Biased shoulder blades, being "out at the elbows," and loose shoulder muscles will cause the latter fault.

Dogs which have a bow to the forearm, or pasterns which turn out from joint to pad will not operate on a straight column of bones. These dogs, as well as the wide-set ones, are not expected to move at high rates of speed nor work for long hours at their top speed. The dog with the turned-out or slue foot can rotate that inward by the *pronator-teres* muscle passing from the humerus to the radius, and not possessed by the horse.

STATIC BALANCE IN THE REAR

Static balance in the back assembly, viewed from the rear, will allow the back legs to stand practically perpendicular to the ground because the joints of the pelvis

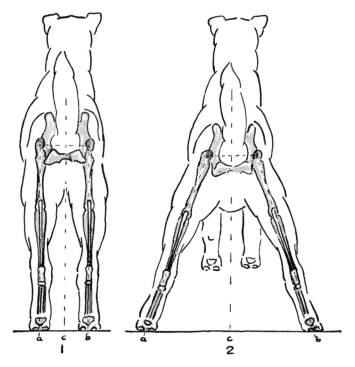

STATIC BALANCE from the rear is accomplished by getting the heel pad directly under the Pelvis Joint, for it is from one to the other that weight passes. 1) A Fox Terrier in static balance; for kinetic balance a would converge on c in single tracking. 2) This dog is in an exaggerated back spread often seen in show rings for this breed and others; this dog is in balance if ac equals cb but it is not complete static balance. The value of the "spread" is to lower the croup in regard to the 'withers' and straighten out the back line, cover such faults as may exist there, and give the dog an aggressive attitude. The working animal is evident in the first animal for they are both the same.

are spread apart so that they usually permit this stand. In kinetic balance or moving, the back legs should move on the same line that is made by the front legs. If any deviation is made they should move closer to the center line in those dogs that cannot come in with the front legs because of low-set, broad chest when the speed dictates. In this and at all times they should "move straight forward when traveling," and not swing in an arc or have the hocks show in or out in regard to this line of travel.

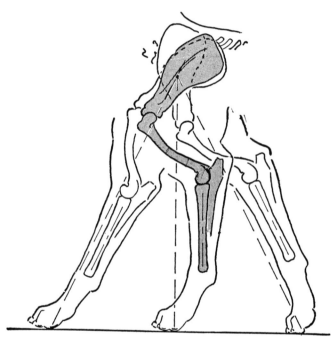

KINETIC BALANCE of the front leg as considered from the side follows closely that of static. The power or force is transmitted from the ground contact through the center of the shoulder blade along a line parallel to the radius, the weight carrier, of the forearm. This relation is maintained from beginning to end of the stride in a kinetically balanced front.

The effort to get leg movement "straight forward" is to utilize all energy along the line of locomotion and not waste it with side trips. At any time we see evidence of these side trips, we can feel certain there is some structural condition causing it. When some dogs are built for special purposes, this condition may be a natural result but otherwise it will be a major fault.

The single-tracking dog, which picks his feet off the ground, will not hit or interfere with the leg that is then bearing weight as this leg is angled inward, and the forward-moving leg can step over it. If the dog does not do this and does interfere, then the leg action is not flexible or spontaneous enough and you can look for a structural or conditional fault.

Up to this point we have treated more with static balance, balance without movement, than kinetic which deals with forces in motion. This was particularly true when discussing the balanced front as viewed from the side. One reason for this is that the application of force absorbed by the front in motion is relatively along the same line, when viewed from the side, as that exerted by supporting the body.

Therefore a front that is in static balance in this plane is quite apt to be in kinetic balance under movement. If that was not the case, we would not have gone to such effort to impress the value of static balance and the things that affected it for the dog is rarely standing still.

The dog which is not statically balanced in front may at times move in kinetic balance if its pasterns are sufficiently flexible. "At times" is the proper expression because he will not maintain it very long. Perhaps this does not make any difference to the house pet for when he gets tired he can curl up for a nap on the rug. On the other hand, it might be just as important and just as much fun to have the body structure of our pet right as to have his eyes and ears right.

As kinetic balance deals with movement, we might see what happens to this front when the dog does move.

In the forward movement of the front leg, the shoulder blade rotates forward on its static center for approximately 15 degrees. The humerus is drawn forward until the knob on its head strikes the nose of the blade socket. The triceps straighten the elbow point as much as possible and the muscles of the forearm contract and put tension on pastern and pad. In this position, the pad strikes the ground, taking the shock on the heel.

This shock is passed up the column of bones to the shoulder blade and is first received by it somewhat in reverse of the normal muscular action, for the shoulder joint is driven upward. The forward half of the *trapezius*, between the top of the blade and neck ligament, and the after part of the *serratus*, between the bottom of the blade and the back ribs, take the action in tension rather than their normal compression. They first act as a brake to keep the blade from moving too far and then by instant reflexive action contract. As soon as the blade starts to rotate backward, the tension is taken up by the other parts of these muscles for the rest of absorption.

By this action, the head of the blade is not driven straight into the muscle assembly like a battering ram, but is handled much as a baseball player takes the shock of a caught ball by letting the glove ride with the force. All of this action, even as the blade continues its backward movement is on the same center that was set up by static balance.

The leg itself begins to contract; the pastern goes down, the elbow bends, and the humerus head rotates in the shoulder socket as the dog's body passes over the pad anchorage. When the blade's center of gravity passes this

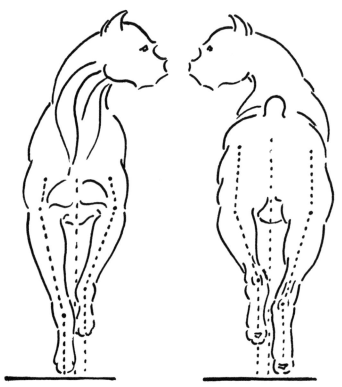

SINGLE TRACKING and moving close are often confused. The close mover coming toward you will converge his pasterns so that the straight line of bone support is broken; sometimes the convergence causes interference. Quite often this pastern will break inward as soon as weight is applied. The fault may show in one or both legs.

THE CLOSE MOVER going away will show the hocks converged often as much or more than the pads. The support by a straight column of bones is broken and the joint may give way either inward or outward; this always offers interference to the opposite leg causing it to swing wide. The fault may show in one or both legs and is sometimes referred to as "dusting a hock."

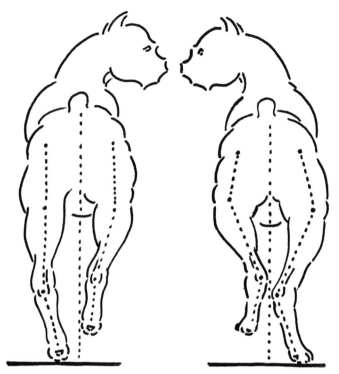

One of the common faults in movement "out of line"
is for the hocks to be deflected outward, though the
leg is traveling in a straight line fore and aft. They
may not show outward bend until weight is applied and
then it may be evidenced in one leg only. This may
show when the dog is standing or only when gaited.
The cow-hocked dog, shown to the right, is a different
animal. The center plane of his leg action below hip
or stifle moves at an angle to the line of progress so
that the hocks are directed inward. This generally shows
at all times though it may not be evident except in action.

pad, the leg straightens, relifts the body, and adds its
contribution to locomotion.

The straightening action comes as the shoulder assembly passes the peak of the arc and starts to fall, taking us
back to "walking is falling." If the action stopped at the

completion of straightening much of its value would be lost. That is a mechanical fact not always easy to explain.

In case you play golf, try checking the driver the moment after its impact with the ball. Swing a baseball bat and do not make any effort to continue its arc after the ball has been hit. Then duplicate these actions with a complete and unbroken follow-through of club and bat. Those experiments will do more than words to convey the value of the leg continuing the sweep of its arc beyond the time that it has straightened and apparently delivered all its punch.

Up to now we have been talking about the front end of the dog most of the time. It has to work perfectly for that kind of results. Like the hands on the clock; but the clock needs something behind the face to put the tick there and make the hands go around. That is likely the other end of the dog.

14

The Back Leg

THERE is a vast difference between the function and purpose of the front and back legs of all four-footed animals. While the front fights to maintain the normal center of gravity, the back leg is continually upsetting it. It is by this action that locomotion is accomplished, and it results in an unending battle between the two assemblies.

Several years ago we were lounging in the cartway of that now extinct institution, the livery stable. Our chairs, with slats where once had been cane seats, were tilted back against the wall of the tack room. On that strip of hard-trod clay, the problems of the world had been solved and the scandals of the community dissected. One of these great discourses was interrupted as Slim led a filly by us.

"Take up on that hackamore line and keep that filly's head up," Uncle Ned barked, "er she's sure to fire a kick."

"How come a horse gets his head down to kick?" asked one of the town sports as he dusted off a chair and pulled up his peg-tops to take a rest.

"He gets set for more push," a colored swipe offered.

"Gets weight off the backhand," Uncle Ned said as he continued platting a whip. "That helps him put the motion in locomotion."

The back leg was not built to carry weight and it operates to the best advantage with as little comparative weight as possible on it either for a kick or to throw push into his motion.

You can check this by pressing down on your dog's loin or croup and then on the withers to compare the difference in stability of the two. It is such a foregone conclusion that the back assembly will give down that it has always seemed rather useless to make the test. The spring back may reveal the quality of the reflex.

Unlike the flexible attachment of the forequarters, the back leg attachment is positive and suffers little mechanical loss in power transmission. The foundation of the assembly is the pelvis or croup, as we designate it externally. This is fixed firmly to the spinal column and our first consideration of it is the angle at which it slopes.

FORCE OF THE BACK LEG

The force of the back leg is transmitted along the longitudinal line of the center of gravity. Physically it goes from the back leg to the spinal column. The laws of kinetics show that a force is more effective if transmitted through two angles rather than through one, particularly one as abrupt as 90 degrees or even 120 degrees. There is also less loss of power if the angles are of equal degree.

When the assembly is static, it is merely supporting body weight and the action is vertical to the spinal column. If that were the full mission of the rear, then the pelvis slope of 45 degrees would be ideal with the change going through two angles of 135 degrees each.

This assembly, though, is not designed to support weight. That is why horsemen keep the saddle forward on the withers whether they want speed or just an old plodder. It is designed to generate power—sometimes for speed, sometimes for pull, sometimes for normal locomotion as is the case with most dogs.

The actual power delivered by the back leg is in ratio to the difference between its extended and contracted lengths during the stride. In other words, the shortest and longest length from stifle to pad during the action of the leg in the stride. This is a fact that must be kept in mind as we look into the various features of the leg and consider their effect upon the gait.

In the full stroke, the leg is carried forward to contact the ground at a point to which momentum takes it and preferably where momentum is exhausted. At this time

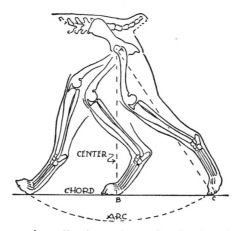

Actually the pad remains fixed and the pelvis is carried forward, but figuratively the action is along a chord of an arc described by the leg action. During the first half of the chord, the leg receives concussion, but from B to C it is transmitting power generated by the rearing muscles. Efficiency is in ratio to the difference between AB and AC, the contracted and extended lengths.

the leg is extended, the speed or gait governing the amount, with muscles taut to receive the shock. The heel pad is the first to strike the ground and take the shock; the toes do not come into play until weight moves up over them and the backward action starts.

The leg begins to contract at both hock and stifle as it is drawn to the rear and does so until the pad is directly under the vertical center of the pelvis socket. Up to this point it has been lifting the forward part of the body somewhat, through the action of the rearing muscles, and getting set for its own push.

From the center vertical back, the leg is delivering power or push. The first prime factor in its ability to do this is the difference in length at the vertical and when fully extended at the completion of the stroke. Another factor is the set of the croup which will govern the amount that the thigh can be drawn back and therefore limits the complete back stroke.

Although the pad is a fixed pivot on the ground, it figuratively travels along a chord of an arc which is described by a radius centered at the hip joint. The chord is limited between the intersections of the arc with the ground. The leg should be able to travel from end to end of this chord but may not, due to set of pelvis and lack of angulation, length of bones and muscles.

SLOPE OF THE CROUP

When the peak of this push is reached, the directional change is not 90 degrees but approaching 120 degrees. Therefore a pelvis slope of 30 degrees with the changes through two 150-degree angles is indicated. Such a slope has been proven afield and adapted by many breeds because it functioned to the best advantage. You will find it to be about standard in good horses.

A deviation from this can be designated as *steep* or *flat*. Each such deviation has advantages for certain purposes and disadvantages for others. In the standard animal, though, they should be considered faults.

We recall a conversation once heard in the office of a Maryland stock farm where polo ponies and hunters were stabled and trained. It was a day following one of those many disposal sales that are held around race tracks.

"Why didn't you buy that chestnut mare yesterday?"

one of the farm's patrons asked. "She looked like a good polo prospect to me."

Without looking up from the feed bills on his desk, the owner replied, "Too flat in the croup for me."

"You're pretty cranky about croups."

"Not cranky—just don't like flat ones on my polo ponies. You know how hard it is to bring a pony around that has to do most of his turning on the forehand. You

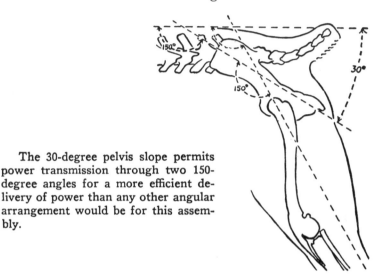

The 30-degree pelvis slope permits power transmission through two 150-degree angles for a more efficient delivery of power than any other angular arrangement would be for this assembly.

played one like that last Sunday and Nick, on that little 'goose rump,' was always about and into line before you were halfway around."

"Then you want them 'goose rumped'?"

"They've got to be that or nearly so to turn on the rearhand with head up rather than box themselves around on their front legs. That's what makes cow ponies give you nine cents change out of a dime."

A steep croup enables a dog to get his feet under him and turn more quickly. The forward reach from this croup draws the weight to the rearhand, forces the rearing muscles into action, lets the back feet act as the pivot on the turn, directs the force more vertically. The hind-quarters with this type croup will compensate somewhat for a front that does not have enough lift to support the center of gravity.

It is an advantage in backing up, and a terrier might find it an aid in backing out of a hole with its prey. Many good "pit dogs," slightly steep in the croup, found this beneficial in delivering the *coup de grace,* which action is almost identical with that of a horse "throwing his weight into the collar" on a snap pull. You find many slow but powerful draft horses with steep croups.

Some breeders of gazehounds apparently want the assistance of this in lifting the center of gravity without some of its disadvantages. They seek an arch in the dog's back so that the whole assembly can be directed forward as though the croup were steep and still permit the leg a full arc of action which a flat croup provides. As the after-half of the arc is the one from which the push comes, this is naturally shortened by the steep croup. That is why you never see them on winners of the Kentucky Derby or the Preakness.

The *flat croup* increases the length of action behind the vertical which puts the real snap in locomotion. It also increases the length of muscles that run from it to the stifle joint and draw the leg backward. These are a part of the rearing muscles and must be good for the dog to move with power.

LENGTHENING THE THIGH MUSCLES

There are three other means of lengthening these mus-cles besides a flat croup. One is a high tail-set because several of them originate directly or indirectly on the fused vertebrae in front of the tail. If the latter is de-pressed, these muscles are shortened. The set of the tail is also a good indicator as to how the pelvis is angled for the relation of the two tend to be uniform.

Another means is lengthening the pelvis bones behind the hip joint. This gives not only longer but wider and stronger muscles. Many Thoroughbreds and the majority of Arabian horses have this part of the pelvis well developed. The rabbit is an emphatic illustration of this char-

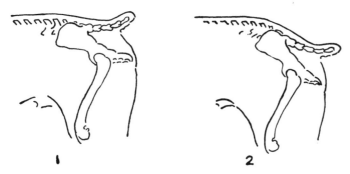

The set of the pelvis on a flat and steep croup is indicated in sketches 1 and 2 revealing the effect this has on the outline of the dog, which is what we see.

acteristic. The length of its pelvis behind the hip joint is extremely long in comparison with the front section. The cat and many other felines are similar in this respect and we are well aware of their ability to get push out of their back legs.

The third method is to lengthen the femur or thigh bone. This is the influence behind every request for *well bent stifles*, but runs into a natural heritage difficulty which causes the bones between the stifle and hock to shorten as this one lengthens. In both the front and back leg we have this trouble, which was long ago recognized by horsemen.

Lacog, a French authority of the last century, says of the horse's front leg, "The length of the forearm varies inversely with that of the cannon bone." In other words, as one got long the other became shorter. He also pointed out that you could go through several thousand horses, pick up the front hoof, and the heel of it would touch the elbow in the same place regardless of the knee location. This tends to show that nature has her own ideas about bone relation and tries to balance them out to that idea.

THE WELL BENT STIFLE

We believe that the majority of fanciers think of a *well bent stifle* as one in which the inside angle between the thigh and the bones below it is around 45 degrees. This means that both sets of bones have to be proportionately long and, gaining this end, we have defeated the natural tendency for them to run inversely. Too much stress cannot be put on the well bent stifle where speed is desired. It is not so much value to draft animals.

The general tendency of the thigh is to assume a position of 90 degrees to the line of the pelvis. In that, its angle to the ground is influenced by the set of the pelvis and with a flat croup to become rather perpendicular to the ground and prevent a well bent stifle. A more generally efficient position is one in which the thigh sets at a 45-degree angle to the ground regardless of croup angle. This invariably means a longer bone and provides a better angle between it and the lower bones or second thigh.

The well bent stifle is as important to the rest of the leg as to the thigh for it means a long second thigh (tibia and fibula), those bones running down to the hock joint, which provide a long Achilles tendon and its muscle that activates the hock joint by attachment to the calcis. Perhaps this is the most important of the entire assembly. Many successful horse trainers pick their yearlings on the length of the tibia, the width of the gaskin (hock joint) and the shortness of the cannon-bone below the hock.

These muscles must hold a balance of power with those

of the rest of the assembly and they are much smaller. Anything we do to increase their length, strength and tone is an advantage to all animals. Definitely they must have

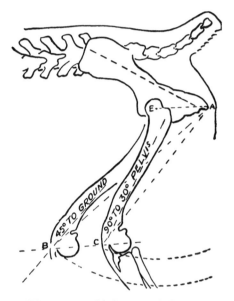

The upper thigh, set 45 degrees to the ground on a 30-degree pelvis (B-E), will usually be longer of bone than one set 90 degrees to the pelvis (C-E), both of which are found in dogs. The former provides longer muscles (B-A) tnan the latter (C-A). However, set C-E is apt to be more enduring aneid and conform more closely to tne front of the average dog. Muscle length and efficiency can also be increased by lengthening the after part of the pelvis (E-A).

the power to straighten the hock joint. That is why horsemen ask for a "straight dropped hock" or for horses to stand "well up on hocks" for in this position it is straight. We know it will bend but do we always know that it can be straightened?

THE SICKLE HOCK

If the dog is *sickle hocked,* standing with a perpetual bend in them, he may not be able to straighten them for one of several reasons. The muscle activating the hock may not be long enough to provide sufficient contraction

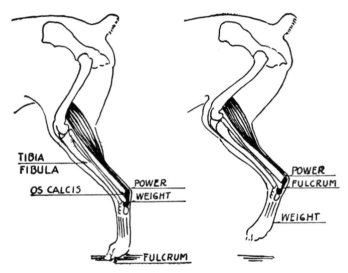

TIBIA
FIBULA
OS CALCIS
POWER
WEIGHT
FULCRUM
POWER
FULCRUM
WEIGHT

THE HOCK JOINT is activated by a muscle and the Achilles tendon which probably does more work than any other in the motive groups. This should be as long as possible to give a complete range of movement to the Hock and Foot. Note how the order of levers change from PWF, when the leg is applying drive, to PFW when it is lifted from the ground. The main mission of the Achilles tendon is to straighten the hock.

for straightening the joint, or cartilage formation may build up in the assembly and prevent complete action. The sickle hock, if forced on the dog by a long column of bones above and below, does promise a greater difference between the extended and contracted length of the leg. Acutely bent stifles are often accompanied by sickle hocks, because of bone ratio and to get the supporting pad under the vertical center of gravity in the assembly.

The German Shepherd is a good example of the sickle hock, for nearly all of them have this feature. For them, it is a natural accompaniment to the acute angulation sought in these animals. If the Shepherd did not stand or move in the slow gaits with a sickle hock, the back pad would not be under the vertical center of gravity and the weight of the body would be carried on the toes and not the heel pad. The main thing to check in this case is the hock's ability to open and provide as nearly as possible a straight line from pad to stifle when the leg completes the arc of action, particularly at high speed.

HOCKS WELL LET DOWN

The request for *hocks well let down,* which is synonymous with *hocks close to the ground* as used by horsemen, is another means of asking for a long set of bones between stifle and hock (tibia and fibula) as well as a short set from hock joint to ground. We know that nature is going to battle us in changing the actual length of the leg so, if we shorten the bones below the hock joint, nature will try to lengthen those above it.

Hocks *well let down* improve the leverage action as regards endurance. In the action of the hock joint, the pad is the fulcrum (F), the weight (W) comes where the tibia and fibula rests on the tarsal bones, and power (P) is applied to the tip of the *os calcis.* Therefore according to the laws of leverage getting the joint close to the ground will lessen the amount of power required to move weight but will not move it as far with the same given power.

Great sprinters do not as a rule have hocks well let down, which is a condition purely comparative with the length of other bones. On the cheetah the distance from hock to pad is about the same as from hock to stifle. The same is true of a rabbit. The deer and the antelope have exceptionally long bones in this section. The pronghorn is extremely high on the hock and is likely our fastest four-footed animal and still has endurance. Where endurance does show up, the *os calcis* is relatively long also which counteracts the fatiguing element without reducing action.

The whole assembly from hock to pad is very important

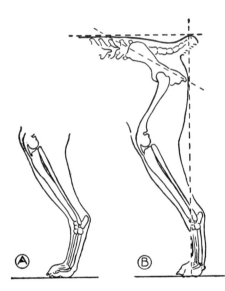

A) SICKLE HOCK, a decided fault unless' Achilles tendon can straighten it. B) An example of "standing well up on hocks" and, incidentally the best position for examining set of pelvis and upper thigh.

in dogs, or in any animal for that matter. In the course of conversation with an old horseman, we once asked: "What are the two most important features on a horse? In other words, if you were buying horses and could see only two parts of the animal, which two would you require?"

"Never thought of it that way," the old man said and then pondered the thought as he watched the curl of smoke from his pipe. "Well," he finally continued, "I guess it would be the shoulder blade in front and the gaskin-cannon bone in the rear. If those two things are right, the rest of the horse is likely right."

That is as true of dogs as horses.

We used to spend a lot of time with old Jake McConnell, who bred some of the best hounds of the Middle West. One day we saw him culling puppies and he was

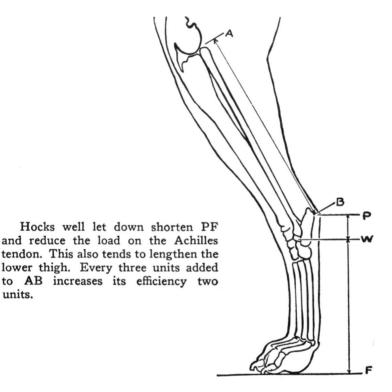

Hocks well let down shorten PF and reduce the load on the Achilles tendon. This also tends to lengthen the lower thigh. Every three units added to AB increases its efficiency two units.

doing it exclusively by the comparative length of hock to pad.

"How does it work?" I asked him.

He shifted a long dead cigar to the corner of his mouth. "Mebbe this ain't the reason—but the longens seem to have a lot of early speed while the shortens are running the next morning."

We watched this on a race a few nights later. The moon was full, one of those all night fulls of October.

There had been a slight shower in the afternoon but the air was still which made it an ideal night for running fox.

Jake put down eight dogs of his own and four belonging to a neighbor. "I ain't got a real good strike dog in the lot," Jake explained, "so we gotta get Butcher and his Triggs. Mine are jump and running dogs. You wanna watch them hocks—all right, there's Topper and Bugle, they're shortens and King's a longen. You just see what happens."

About 9:30 the Triggs made a strike and worked it out, then a few minutes later they had jumped Old Red and the race was on. For the next four hours it sounded almost like a one-dog race. It was King out there telling the world about it. He had a clear screaming mouth that could be heard for miles up and down the valley. During this time the fox had taken them down one ridge and was bringing them back the other.

Old Red must have been a powerful animal for those dogs were really giving it to him. The race was unusually fast. You knew that King was close enough to be running by body scent and not trailing but he still had not put that note in his tongue that says, "I'm right on your tail." Some of the dogs had already begun to say they had enough and we could expect them to come straggling in before long.

"I haven't heard Topper and Bugle yet," I said, "or have I?"

"Naw, you ain't heard 'em since a few minutes after the jump. They're both free mouth dogs when they get in the right place but they don't do a lot of wrong talking."

Then here came the fox, still running tail high, cutting across a long field next to us and heading back for the other ridge. He was smart for that was a cornfield and the ground was soft and loose. He would sail over it without sinking in much while it would act like a brake to all the dogs.

King was still leading the pack. Topper and Bugle were up pretty close but not enough to open. Then just as they went into the ridge we heard them, both of them probably running almost shoulder to shoulder. It was a rolling note, strong and full, that contrasted markedly with King's scream.

"There they are," said Jake with satisfaction, "that's all you'll hear from now to sun-up."

He was right. When Red finally went to a hole about two miles down the valley, after taking them around the circuit again, Topper and Bugle were the only two dogs giving him a race, the rest had come in and had been stowed away in the cars.

So we still remember Jake's advice—"longens for early speed, shortens to keep on going."

THE BACK PAD

The dog's back pad is usually smaller than the front one. We do not know whether nature figured it that way but it does reduce fatigue elements. To increase the size of it, though, would impart greater speed. This increase should be accomplished mostly by the lengthening of the third digit to give more leverage action as was pointed out in the discussion of the cat- and hare-feet.

Though both front and back feet should be compact and firm of muscular tension, this condition is more important to the back than front foot. The greatest force which hits the front pad is that of concussion and is taken through the heel pad. The back pad is subjected to its greatest effort at the peak of its drive when the toes are definitely in the action. For that reason, it is more important for the muscles and tendons controlling them to be in top condition and that means a firm compact foot on examination.

A number of standards emphasize that *hocks should not be turned in nor out.* Very few dogs will turn them out and, if so, they are turning their pads inward to a pigeon-

If the dog's hocks incline inward rather than point directly back in line with the body, he is cow-hocked; the term is derived from cows which are all built this way. Leg action is on a bias to line of travel and loses efficiency in ratio to this deviation.

toed position—these dogs are usually slack in loin. Lack of clearance for the stifle to work will push the stifle out and the hocks inward to the cow-hocked position. Occasionally dogs are structurally cow-hocked even as the cow.

Either of these positions takes the action of the leg out of the straight forward line and applies power on a bias to the line of locomotion, losing efficiency. Though cow-hocked oxen will out-pull horses weight for weight and there have been a few stake winners on the track with them, they should be considered faults.

POSITION FOR EXAMINATION

The best position for examining the true angulation of the rear assembly is to pose the dog so that a perpendicular line dropped from the point of the buttock coincides with the front line of the bones below the hock joint. See illustration on page 200. If we were judging this for weight-carrying or static balance we would place the pad on the vertical center of gravity. We are interested in its kinetic balance and its ability to produce motion, therefore, we place the pad so that the features contributing to this are made clear. This position, evolved by French horsemen years ago, is time tested for its revelation of what we have in the animal without distortion.

In this position the pelvis should show its 30-degree angle with the bones below the hock joint standing vertical and the stifle taking whatever angle it possesses. If the pad is carried forward it will induce more bend in the stifle and may steepen the croup and also make the dog show sickle hocked.

The usual practice in the show ring is to stretch the back legs behind this position which flattens the back line and the croup as well as straightens the stifle. If the back or loin is roached and the croup steep, this will somewhat cover these faults. The stretched position also suggests alertness which adds to the appearance of the dog but does not give us as true a view of his back assembly. Dogs which are alert will often assume a position with a degree of stretch as a natural course if their assemblies are kinetically balanced, for they are more at ease in this position.

15

The Spinal Column

THE delivery and receiving end of the dog must be tied together; this is done by the spinal column which can be likened to the truss bays of a cantilever or the cables of a suspension bridge. In addition to serving as the link between the fore and after assemblies, the spinal column also supports the organs and structure of the body.

From an anatomical and mechanical viewpoint, the column is divided into several sections, each of which serves a specific purpose. There is often confusion as to the limits of these divisions. No standard gives them a specific definition; some are ambiguous, obscure and vague on the subject. The course of the spinal column is revealed to us by the top line of the dog; some call this "back" from stem to stern, others chop it up into uncertain parts.

For instance, one standard says, . . . *the length of back equal to shoulder height* . . . Another will say, *The back strong and straight . . . the loin slightly arched.* Others will give us two headings and descriptions: one for the back and one for the loin. For our purpose, we will have to sort these ideas out and get on one track with them so that we will know what part of this spinal column we are talking about when a designation is used.

If "back" is to be "back line," it cannot be straight and level and still have slightly arched loins, neither can it have well developed withers, for the spires must be longer there for that. We shall hold to the anatomical division of the spinal column of neck, withers, back, loin, croup, and tail for these are distinctive and have specific work to do.

Though the head is not a specific part of the spinal column, we will give it consideration at this point for it does affect the action of the neck. Aside from the individual characteristics which tell you more or less the animal's breed, the action of the head is quite important to locomotion.

THE HEAD AND NECK

The head and neck together shift the center of gravity from side to side in turns, raise and depress it, and give the major influence in maintaining equilibrium. When

THE BORZOI HEAD is long and streamlined for speed; it is built on the same general lines as all other gazehounds.

running, the dog extends the head and neck forward to put more weight on the forehand and create greater instability, thus increasing speed. If the dog wants to stop quickly, head and neck will go up throwing the center of gravity backward and acting as a counter brake. Long heads and long necks move the center of gravity forward more than short heads and necks. Momentum will increase their influence on this center.

The general structure of the head will depend on breed and purpose. The streamlined head of the gazehounds

THE GERMAN SHEPHERD HEAD, like that of the Pointer and the Setter, is of medium length without emphatic width; a type best suited for continuous work afield without emphasis on speed.

with the ears folded to reduce wind resistance are logically a benefit to speed. This characteristic is more important to them than their ability to bite. The ability to bite, however, is very much affected by the dog's fill-in before the eyes. The maxillary bone on each side of the bridge of the nose backs up the molars. A snipy, pinched face will not have molars set in a good foundation. The tooth root will either be short or inclined inward so that biting exerts a leverage action instead of a straight thrust.

Terriers, hounds, retrievers or any dog handling heavy objects, retrieving or fighting game should have a well developed maxillary skeleton. There should never be a compromise with a snipy face.

Dogs which work trail scent or retrieve objects from

THE BOXER HEAD is short of face providing a strong bite due to the short leverage employed. This type of head set back into the body by a short neck, as on the Bulldog, moves the center of gravity to the rear.

the ground require a neck and head length which, combined, permits nose and mouth to reach the ground without forcing the dog into a stooped position—working on his knees. Almost universally we find that head and neck are related to one another in length; the short or broken faced dogs will have a relatively short neck, while the long heads of the Wolfhound and Whippet possess the long neck.

The neck with its seven vertebrae comes in for its share of balance with the head. The neck really should be considered a part of the forequarters for it is definitely an integral part of that. All of the muscles which draw the leg forward depend on the neck for base support directly or indirectly.

You might divide the neck into two parts: from the pole

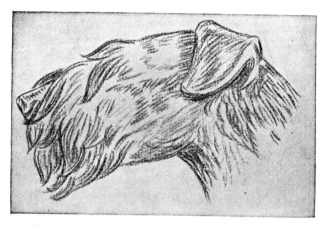

THE KERRY BLUE has a typical terrier head and must possess a firm, hard bite with dentition well backed up by the skull. It should closely resemble a rectangle when viewed from the side.

forward and backward. Forward we have only two vertebrae but to these are affixed the long strips of muscles running down from each side to attach themselves to the upper arm and draw it forward. With the head held high, these tend to "lift" the action, but when the head is extended the direction of pull is more specifically in the line of travel. These are the muscles with which the dog shakes its prey—the feet remain firm and they act from side to side.

If the pole has a definite indication in the back line of the neck, the dog has much better control of his front action and is not nearly so apt to stumble. Any good horse-man can tell you the advantage of "breaking the pole" of a horse's neck when riding him—it not only gives you, as the rider, better control of the horse but the horse is far more certain in handling himself.

Behind the pole, we should have an efficient neck liga-ment. First the spires of the neck and spinal vertebrae

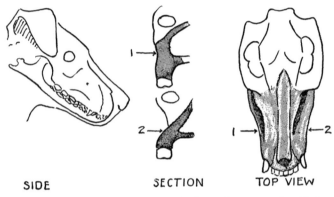

SIDE   SECTION   TOP VIEW

THE TERRIER SKULL before the eyes should be well filled in to give proper molar support. In the section view, the back-up of the molars is shown by comparing sketches 1 and 2. Top View shows a good fill-in (1) as compared with a snipy face (2).

must be large to give firm anchorage to the ligament threads. "Large" in this sense is relative and does not mean that the Scottie's should compare with the Dane's. High, prominent withers, particularly if the spinal col-umn runs level in front of the loin, indicates a wide thick ligament for its main body will fill the triangular space be-tween the pole, base and tip of the first dorsal vertebra.

The *ewe* or concave neck shows weakness of the neck ligament, inability to control the break of the pole and provides very poor support to the muscles moving the front leg forward. This is usually followed by a tendency to or an actual sway back. *Bull necks,* except in the breeds that are patterned for them, shorten the length and action of muscles controlling the shoulder blade and the forward movement of the leg.

Where speed is a question, we will take the long head and neck but, if we prefer endurance, a head and neck of medium length and weight will do a better job. The dogs that go to ground for their game can do with more head than neck or at least the two of equal length.

Perhaps no single part of the dog more definitely establishes his adherence to a breed pattern in the eyes of the usual and often schooled observer than does the head, its expression and make-up. Aside from the general picture that you like to see, much information can be taken from the head alone, for we have many linked heritage characteristics such as color of eyes and ability to hear, ear length and scenting faculty.

THE EARS

Sometimes we might say that the ears make the head. It is safe to say that Fox Terrier judges would have consistently put the great Nornay Saddler down had his ears been fly instead of button. This would not have been as serious structurally as herring gut or shoulder blades on his neck. It would have taken him out of the picture pattern set as the standard even as the vertical shoulder blade does. However, the judge often overlooks a body fault but rarely a head fault; perhaps because it stares him in the face all the time.

While heads are definitely the hallmark or characteristic stamp of any specific breed, a good specimen will vary in many details from time to time and group to group due to personal preferences. Many things enter into this: personal opinion, the head that happens to accompany a breeding line that is improving some other feature, but more specifically the head that by chance is on the dogs

CHARACTERISTIC EAR TYPES

PENDANT — DALMATIAN

TRIMMED-SCHNAUZER

LEATHER — BEAGLE

PENDULOUS-COCKER

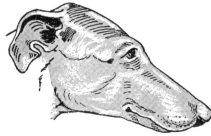

ROSE — WHIPPET

BUTTON HOOD — PUG

CHARACTERISTIC EAR TYPES

BUTTON –FOX TERRIER   PRICK–SCOTTY

BAT – BASENJI   SEMI-PRICK —COLLIE

belonging to the kennels which are doing most of the winning or on your own dogs.

These variations usually embody such things as the exact tilt of the nose, the size and placement of the eye, profile outline, number of wrinkles, size and set of ears, and so on. Variations generally are slight but enough to change expression and make one Greek look like another Greek. Heads come and go in style like my lady's hats and to say which one is the better is like choosing a pretty girl—Jim goes head-over-heels for a tip-tilted nose while a classic acquiline gives John goose pimples.

Therefore the style of heads is a discussion we try to avoid. Any style is good so long as it is characteristic of the breed, functions efficiently in the life and purpose of the dog and does not upset the required balance of the individual. At no time though should style variation in a head be considered as more important than the functional structure and conformation of the animal.

We find at least ten characteristic ears on the various dog heads with some variations of these. In some cases they are primarily for expression while others do have a working factor in their design. The scent faculty is related somewhat to length of leather in the ear. Open ears, whether trimmed or of the prick type, offer less obstruction to hearing. Dogs working by scent alone though may be distracted from this line of work by hearing unrelated sounds. Generally the type of ear best suited for the work has become the fashion on the dog.

Long necks indicate long and in some cases broad muscles going from it to the front assembly. However, long necks are usually thin and provide muscles of relative character that will lack strength. By giving the dog a comparatively long neck, you should get an increase in sprinting speed while the opposite contributes to endurance.

THE WITHERS

The withers anatomically are composed of seven vertebrae. The word *withers* is derived from an old Anglo-Saxon word that means "against" or "acting *with* against" and was first used to describe that part of the horse which acts against the collar and then the juncture of the shoulder blades forming an elevation at the springing of the neck. This one single point where the top of the blades almost meet is the common conception of the term. However, we find that the first seven vertebrae are so involved in shoulder action that they, rather than just the single high point, are of importance to the assembly.

These vertebrae differ specifically from those composing the remainder of the column in that they each have a long finger or spinous process thrust upward and angled backward which gives support to neck ligament and the muscles coming from the shoulder blade. These fingers get shorter in length as they progress backward to the eighth. Quite definitely these fingers must have pronounced length to be of the greatest possible value in their work. Unless the spinal column slopes downward as it comes forward from the loin section, taking up valuable space in the thoracic cavity, these spires cannot be long without showing as the highest part of the back line.

As this line of the withers slopes downward, there is often a semblance of a dip indicated at its juncture with the rest of the back line. Instead of it being a fault, as so many may term it, this indicates that the spires are long even though the spinal column may not be setting level. With a downward slope over the withers and a level back there certainly must be a change of direction when the two lines meet.

THE BACK

The back itself consists of six vertebrae. Two of these carry sternal ribs, four of them carry asternal or those not connected directly to the breast bone or sternum. The last rib on each side is normally not connected with the others.

The power generated in the back legs is delivered forward by thrust through the spinal column. There can be no question about a straight column of bones delivering thrust to better advantage than one not straight or taking a deflected course. So wherever other conditions do not dictate a deviation, this spinal column should be straight and pursue a line parallel with the ground when the dog is stationary. That is the main reason for asking that the "back" be level.

The spires of the last six dorsal vertebrae rarely vary in length one from the other, so whatever course their top line takes will indicate the direction of alignment of the main column. As there is nothing forward to deflect this column once it gets started on the right track, a level "back" will tell you where it is going and the length of the withers' spires. For that reason this section of the top line, whether you choose to call it the *back* or not, should be level or parallel to the ground.

When the vertebrae of this anatomical back section are not parallel with the ground, or level if we choose to call it that, we will unquestionably have one of two structural faults. If this section is directed downward, then we do have relatively long spires on the withers' vertebrae but the spinal column is dropping down into the thoracic cavity and stealing room from the lungs, also it is setting the neck support low on the body. Should this section be directed upward toward the withers, then we are getting more lung room at the sacrifice of good anchorage for the muscles attached to the withers.

Though we have no recourse to written records that substantiate the fact, we firmly believe that is what the old gentlemen had in mind when they put the phrase *level back* in many of the older standards. As pointed out, they certainly could not have meant a "level back line" for, almost in the next breath, they demanded an arch in a portion of that. At least, this answer is sound from a mechanical and functional consideration while the "level back line" is not.

THE LOINS

Between the thoracic section and the pelvis or croup, we have the loins, consisting of seven vertebrae. These are longer and wider than the dorsal vertebrae and their

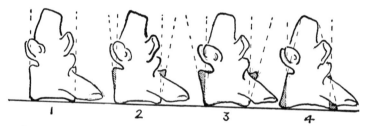

LOIN VERTEBRAE. The keystone arch to the Loin is accomplished through angle taken by the articulating faces of the vertebrae. 1) The faces here are parallel and will give a flat Loin. 2) This is a vertebra from a "slightly arched" Loin, the faces taking a keystone shape. 3) Exaggerated angle to faces found in a "roach" or "camel" Back. 4) Reversing the face angle gives us a "sway" Back. This usually comes first by a sag from weakness and then the faces fill in with cartilage.

spinous processes are short, thin, and wide, being inclined forward to give better support to the action of the dorsi or *rearing muscles* in this vicinity. Their pull is backward while those of the shoulder is forward. Through this section passes the drive of the back legs, the shock of the forehand landing and the power to relift the forehand to normal level or over a fence.

This section does not receive support from other bones of the framework but sets like a bridge or arch between the two business ends. The majority of standards ask for a *slightly arched loin* in an effort to gain the strength that a keystone gives an unsupported span in structural work. This keystone is not provided by simply contracting the muscles and bending the column into an arch, as one might

1   2

1) A Pointer with level Back and arched Loin. 2) This shows the arch coming well into the Back and producing a roach.

a string of beads, but by the actual shape of the vertebrae.

The articular faces of these vertebrae are inclined so that each vertebrae is shorter at the bottom than the top of the face, thus forming a wedge for an arched loin to be structurally right. A sag here, and also at other points of the back line, indicates that these faces are inclined so that the bottom is longer than the top. The original sag might come from the supporting muscles and ligaments becoming weak and then the articular faces filling up with cartilage as they will do in time; a condition that shows up often with age.

The arched loin is not to be confused with the *camel* or *roach back,* both of which are generally as undesirable as *sway* or *soft back.*

The *camel back* more properly describes the back line that starts an arch up around the blade tips and has its highest point where the thoracic and loin vertebrae meet. The *roach back* starts further back along the column, perhaps at the eleventh vertebrae and from that point on arches over the loin into the croup. The terms *wheel back* or *carriage back* are often used for one or both of these variations.

Under certain conditions we cannot escape a curve or

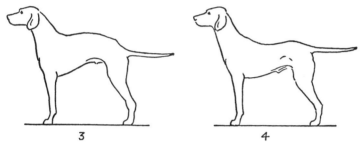

3   4

3) This Pointer has a decided camel back which begins its arch well up into the withers. These dogs are often decidedly "herring gutted." 4) This Pointer has a sway back which is generally accompanied by a ewe neck, also shown.

wheel to the back line regardless of what term we apply to it. Where the croup is higher than the withers, as in the Bulldog, or much lower than the withers, as in the Borzoi, it is necessary for a graceful and efficient back line. A curve in these eliminates the necessity of transmitting power through a single or double sharp angle, using from seven to 15 slight angles instead. The opposite of these terms, *sway back*, describes the upside down arch often seen in old fellows.

Soft backs, those that are not positive and firm when the dogs move, may be actually or potentially inherited; they may indicate poor health or a lack of sufficient exercise to tighten the muscles. These backs are quite apt to sag permanently as the dog grows older.

The keystone arch should be sought in all breeds for the loin section but generally this should not be greater than necessary to provide structural strength. If there is to be a deviation, let it be upward into a roach for these will not sag and become soft as quickly as a loin without any arch.

We might point out here that the exaggerated arch or roach of the loin and back line, with the pronounced tuck-up, so often exhibited on Whippets and other gaze-hounds in the show ring does not seem to be a necessary attribute to their speed. It is an effort to get the action of the back legs well up under the dog and still have a relatively flat croup so that the back action is not choked off by this. However, the majority of Whippets which have established enviable track records have been comparatively flat in back line with just enough loin arch to provide strength to the section.

Greyhounds which bang around track records and win coursing trials usually have a back line sloping down over prominent withers to the seventh or eighth vertebrae, leveling off until a very slight arch is met in the loins. Sometimes these back lines are almost straight from the seventh vertebrae to the horns of the pelvis. Other things notable about them are extremely long bones between stifle and hock, standing well up on hocks, having sufficient bend to the pasterns to give flexibility and prevent knuckling-over, and they cannot be classed as *short coupled*.

The pronghorn antelope has a back line with prominent withers but almost no indication of an arch to the loins and no tuck-up. As he is the fastest of our quadrupeds, we can feel confident that he is not far off the right track on any part of his anatomy when getting over the ground is a consideration.

THE CROUP

The croup, as far as the spine is concerned, extends from the last vertebra of the loin to the first of the tail. These vertebrae have all fused together into a solid member but they still have their spires and projections to which the muscles are attached.

The slope of the croup very accurately indicates the slope of the pelvis for that member is anchored to it and its inner arch rather governs the set of the croup. The angle, however, is controlled by muscular action, particularly those of the loin. You can pinch the loin muscles and the croup will flatten. Paralysis of the loin muscles will also flatten it. Therefore, the flat croup that you see today may indicate weak *rearing muscles* rather than a congenital characteristic.

THE TAIL

The tail is also a barometer to the set of the pelvis and the value of the muscles attached to the pelvis and croup. Furthermore a normal tail or any part of it will tell us several important things about the dog in front of that tail.

Examine a normal tail and you will find that the vertebrae are progressive in size but that the members taper from one juncture to the next and that each one observed will give you a good idea as to what to expect of the next closest one. Just as one bone in the leg will give you a good mental picture of the adjacent one and from there on to the full structure of the dog, the base vertebrae of the tail will tell you volumes about the spinal column. One or two bones taken at random from any animal will enable you to construct a full skeleton of a normal specimen.

Many old-timers picked their dogs by the size of the

TAILS CHARACTERISTIC OF BREEDS

SABER–SHEPHERD   RING–ELKHOUND   PLUME–COLLIE   WHIP–POINTER

DOCKED–BOXER   GAY,CUT–POODLE   CURVED–BORZOI   PLUME–SETTER

BRUSH–CHOW   DOCKED–DOBE   SICKLE–BEAGLE   GAY–SCOTTY

PLUME–PEKE   SCREW–BOSTON   CRANK–BULLDOG   CUT–COCKER

TAIL FAULTS

SET LOW or HIGH   SQUIRREL   WRY   ANY NOT SPECIFIED BY STANDARDS tail at its base. "A dog is no better that his tail," has been said often. Another old time comment was, "A dog thinks with his tail." Certainly its carriage and action indicates the dog's mental attitude.

Two muscles activate the top side of the tail and one the bottom. If the tail is curled, "sickle," or "squirreled" continuously when this is not characteristic, it is not that the top muscles have become more tense but that the one on the bottom has lost or did not have sufficient tension. The tail that takes a corkscrew turn has normal tension on only one of the *lateralis* muscles on top.

These *lateralis* muscles are the continuation of muscles which start at the back of the rib structure and play an important part in tensing the loins. You will note that a dog at play, throwing a gay tail will have slightly more than the usual arch to his loins. The wry or twisted tail indicates that one of the *lateralis* muscles is weak. Unless these conditions have become characteristic over generations, it is safe to conclude that muscles which are not functioning correctly at their terminals are not doing any better along the spinal column.

The length and cross section of all the vertebrae in the spinal column are quite important and should be considered in any dog, particularly those used for breeding. The diameter of the body of the dorsal vertebrae decreases from the first to the eighth, the longest vertical spire coming on the second or third. From the eighth the cross section increases. The lumbar or loin vertebrae decrease in vertical diameter and increase in transverse diameter progressively from the back to the croup.

The ruggedness of these bones provide substantial anchorage for the attached muscles and indicate the size and length of the ribs that spring from the dorsals.

A number of breeds have altered the tails by mutation and developed the drop, hook, kink, rabbit, screw, and spike. One has to watch for one trouble in these: mutation does not always stop where it is visible but tends to cast an influence to bones beyond this point.

The vertebrae of the croup and the pelvis bones are apt to reflect the mutation of the tail and manifest this at whelping and other times. Whatever condition you have in one vertebra will be extended to the next in milder degree. So, if mutation is to be the fashion it is more safely practiced if it is not permitted to enter the last visible vertebra at the base of the tail.

Even as the dog begins with his head, he ends with his tail and by it many a story is told for it expresses health, mental attitude and what may be expected in the rest of the spinal column. Beware of any type tail that is not normally characteristic of the specific breed.

There may be confusion at times as to the number of vertebrae in the dog's tail that has been docked or shortened by mutation. For instance, we see a Doberman and can find evidence of only one or two vertebrae or our Boston shows only two vertebrae in his hook or screw tail. The first few vertebrae of the tail are hidden inside the dog and cannot be seen.

The cocygeal vertebrae which make up the tail begin at the last of the sacral vertebrae to which the pelvis is attached. There are usually three tail vertebrae between the sacral and the first one that comes to view outside the dog and appears as the base of his tail. Therefore the dog that shows only two vertebrae really has five.

16

The Body

Not even the scent of magnolia could be detected on the hot still air over those Southern acres, and the Pointers and Setters fighting it out for the Governor's stake were finding it tough to show class through the two-hour heats. They would go off with the flash character-istic of any dog whose campaign wins over the circuit qualified for this stake but by the last half of the second hour were as burnt up as an unchoked cigarette butt. Bird-finds were few and far between because they were not moving, and scenting is always difficult when the air is hot and dry.

It was the midday brace on the last day of the running which brought out old Jake with his white and liver Pointer, affectionately called Lumber because as a puppy they had kidded him about the dog just lumbering along. During the first hour Lumber barely managed to get up to his fast brace-mate in time to honor his two finds. Then somewhere around the turn of the hour he forged ahead to even the score for bird-work.

Within the last half-hour he went out so far that the judges had to separate to keep each dog under observa-tion. Lumber was not moving any faster now than he had at the start but he was not moving any more slowly, and by contrast it seemed as though he had sped up. In the last five minutes, he checked a long, hard cast, turned sharply and nailed a firm point.

Later when we could congratulate Jake on taking the stake without a second series, we were surprised at his remark.

"Naw, he didn't win on bird-work—you gotta have more'n that to top these stakes," Jake chuckled, his old face masked with the expression of a kid who knew where the jam was hidden. "You know—it was his two ribs that did it."

In that simple statement is far more knowledge of dogs than can be set down in a thousand words. The secret of Lumber's success did lay in two ribs. What Jake had learned by close observation over the years, we shall seek to verify.

Endurance and health depend on the amount of energy supplied to the working parts of the dog. At various points in this discussion, we have emphasized features which reduce the amount required for the movement of a given part. We could get the same working result by stepping up the supply available, for the only advantage of reduction is to prevent requiring more than we can supply.

This energy is generated internally by the organs of the dog, and the housing of those organs is as important as the building around the machines of a factory. These organs had to do the same relative work for Lumber on the parched bird-field as they do for a husky on the ice-bound trails or a Chihuahua on the silk cover of a chaise-longue, that is, manufacture the energy which the dog uses.

Variations in body type for different breeds are super-ficial rather than basic because fundamentally that which makes a good factory building for one animal does the same for another. The law of give and take can no more be escaped here than elsewhere, however, and if we are out for speed we have to be careful lest we leave endur-ance in the kennel and send good health to our country cousin.

The body is divided into two parts: the thorax or

rib section, which houses the heart and lungs; the abdominal, where we find the stomach, the small and large intestines. Regardless of breed or type of dog, these cavities must be of sufficient size, whether deep, wide, long, or what-not, to house these organs and permit them to function efficiently.

THORAX OR RIB SECTION

We secure the dormant or stationary capacity of the thorax to provide heart and lung room by increasing width or depth of the body. Simple; but it does not work that easily. If we want to minimize lateral displacement, which we have found is quite desirable for any animal that must move in the field or on the track, we have to trade width for depth. On the other hand, the dog, which does not have to do much scampering around but needs a low center of gravity and wide base to prevent being upset, can go to the other extreme and take on width. We are thinking now strictly of the space in which the organs are housed and are not asking them to work.

The lungs are carried on both sides of the thorax in two independent lobes. The external faces are convex, smooth and molded snugly against the ribs. The internal or mid-faces form vertical planes between which the stomach tube passes, and the heart is suspended from approximately the mid-point. The after faces of the lungs are molded firm against the diaphragm.

The heart lies on the sternum bone somewhere between the juncture with the sternum of the third and eighth rib. Because of its partial suspension by means of the large vessels entering the lungs, it is directed downward and backward so that the place at which it needs excess room is around the eighth rib where its nose touches the base of the diaphragm.

THE DIAPHRAGM

The diaphragm, one of the most important muscles in the dog's body, separating the thoracic from the abdominal cavity is placed in an oblique direction downward and forward. Its attachments originate on the lumbar or loin vertebrae, thence cutting diagonally down the rib walls

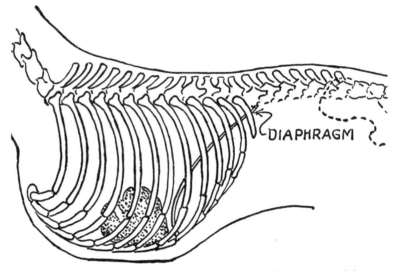

Rib Section. Thirteen pairs of ribs house the heart and lungs. The heart rests on the sternum bone between the third and eighth ribs, and the lungs receive their major activation from the diaphragm muscle. Ample space must be provided for the heart and a long diaphragm is more efficient.

to the seventh rib where it curves back toward the end of the sternum. From the rear it is concave, fitting against the lungs.

The major value of this muscle is to aid breathing. Its concave face flattens out into an oblique plane, creating a vacuum pull on the external face of the lungs, which in turn draws air into the lungs through the bronchial tube. When again it becomes concave the air is forced out of the lungs. Dogs can breath by diaphragm action without the ribs moving.

The muscle can raise the ribs by making the abdominal viscera its fixed point. It can aid the abdominal muscles in expulsive efforts and when affected with irregular spasmodic contractions produces hiccoughs.

We note that the diaphragm's aid to breathing is by creating a vacuum outside the lung's walls. The ribs influence breathing likewise by causing a change in the cubic content of the thoracic cavity. Their design should be such as to make this change the greatest possible for the dog of given size.

Twelve of the 13 ribs on each side have two parts: the main curved body is bone starting from a ball-and-socket seat on a vertebra, and a hard, elongated cartilage that attaches the first nine to the sternum and the next three to the cartilage of the rib immediately in front. There is freedom of action where cartilage meets rib or other cartilage. We might emphasize here that the main value of the rib lies in the bony section.

This bony section forms a compound curve so that when laid flat on the table the two ends will not be in the same plane. The real length of it is not the straight measurement from tip to tip but along its curved surface for that is what creates the action.

The ribs do not expand straight out from the dog's body as though being pushed away from the center line. Instead they pivot on the ball and socket head and the lower cartilage members. Their outward curve does not rest in a plane at right angles to the body but is inclined backward from top to bottom. Therefore, when they rotate forward, by muscular action, air is inhaled; muscular tension is then released and they return, elastically, to the original position and the air is exhaled.

We will recapitulate the salient facts just discussed before analyzing the effect which any physical changes

might have on the function of the rib section. 1) The
lungs set against the rib walls and diaphragm muscle. 2)
The heart lies on the sternum or breast bone between the
third and eighth rib base. 3) The diaphragm muscle runs
obliquely from the loins to the sternum. 4) Ribs do not
expand outward but rotate to change the internal capacity
of the cavity. 5) The change from minimum to maximum
of the thoracic cavity's capacity governs its aid to breathing.

EXPERIMENT ON CAPACITY CHANGE

You might perform an experiment to gain a clearer
view of rib action. Take a small piece of wire—a
straightened hairpin or paper clip—and bend it into the

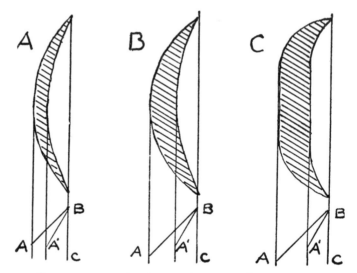

Change of capacity in the thorax section by rib action
can be projected mathematically. Each type shown here
angulates backwards 45 degrees and is rotated 30 degrees.
Each is initially the same distance from the center line or
points of rotation on the spinal column and sternum.
The shaded portion shows the change. A) A flat rib with
no definite "spring." B) Convex or barrel-type rib. C)
Flat sided rib with a good "spring" in initial curves.

arc of a circle. Hold the points of this on the table, inclining the curve at about 45 degrees, and move it to the vertical and then back to the inclined position. The more you incline it, the greater change is effected in the space between it and the table. It can go down until flat for maximum change but such a rib would put a straight side on the dog when dormant and not leave room for the organs.

With the wire lying flat on the table, bend the two ends down toward the table so that they act as legs. Rotate the wire again on its points. You have the rudiments of a compound curve and by its action can see that the ribs could appear flat on the side of the dog—"slab-sided," if you choose—and still produce a decided change in internal capacity if they are well sprung, which is what the bending of the points did.

Straighten the wire again and then bend its two ends down, leaving about one-half the wire straight, and rotate this from a 45-degree incline to a vertical position. This will show the action of a well-sprung rib with a flat midsection that does not interfere with the free action of the shoulder blade and front leg.

The rib itself is not as pronounced in its bends as you have likely made the wire; also it has a corkscrew twist that gets the terminals out of the same plane. However, this experiment should show that we can get change of capacity even from the unsprung "barrel" rib if it is originally turned sufficiently off the plane of its maximum segment. Also that a flat-sided rib section does not mean lack of capacity change.

RIB QUALITY

The length of the bony section of the rib is of utmost importance. Two factors will govern this in addition to the depth of the dog's body: 1) the amount that is actually bone, 2) the angle it takes from its spinal base.

This takes us back to old Jake's remark about Lumber winning the Governor's stake on two ribs. It also brings out the term, *well ribbed up,* which was borrowed from horsemen and was applied by them to the last, floating rib, or the last two or three ribs. The length of these ribs and the angle at which they set will tell us what to expect of the rest of them.

If this last rib springs out well from the spinal column, is of good size and not just a bone splinter, angles backward at 45 degrees, and has good length, the remainder of the ribs will likely follow the same pattern.

We specified a backward angle of 45 degrees, for only that will give us the longest possible rib fitting into the vertical space in the given dog's body which can be taken up without changing the actual size of the body. The thickness of one bone indicates the thickness of the adjacent bone. The length of one bone will also indicate the length of the same type bone next to it.

The ideal rib is angled backward to give it its greatest possible length, has a bony section long in comparison to its cartilage ending, well-sprung in the initial outward curve from the spinal column, and angled backward off the transverse plane to produce a maximum change in the area of its segment when rotated. The mid-section of the rib can be flat or "barrelled" as the type of dog or its location on the body might indicate.

The first four or five ribs should not have as much spring or curve as the remainder and be definitely flat-sided to give greater freedom to the action of the shoulder blade.

BODY DEPTH

Body depth should not be measured behind the elbows but vertically through the head of the ninth rib. It has long been the practice of horsemen to make this measurement from the lowest part of the back which is where the vertebrae of the withers taper off. This will give us a true idea as to heart room. The brisket line should run parallel to the ground back to the base of the eighth or ninth rib. If it starts sweeping up at the third or fourth,

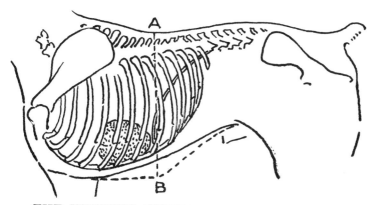

THE HERRING GUTTED DOG, whose bottom line sweeps upward too quickly, is robbed of heart and lung room as well as of length of diaphragm. He is never a good stayer afield. Body depth should be measured vertically through the head of the ninth rib or the tip of the sternum, not just behind the elbows. This sketch shows a herring gutted dog whose base line should have followed the broken line.

as is so often seen, the heart will be robbed of room and pushed up between the lungs, curtailing their action also.

Horsemen term this quick upsweep of the brisket *herring gut*, and the condition is looked upon as an unforgivable fault. It not only takes away heart and lung room but materially shortens the span of the diaphragm muscle.

A dog can have *tuck-up* without being herring gutted if the upsweep does not start in front of the diaphragm base anchor or heart section. For maximum heart and lung room, tuck-up must confine itself to the abdominal section. The value of this is evident when we take a good look at dogs, horses and other animals which do a good continuous job of covering ground. The stake horses, Irish hunters, big-going field trial Pointers and Setters, Greyhounds that win the cups on the tracks and good movers of the wild will all show a high percentage of specimens with a long, level brisket line.

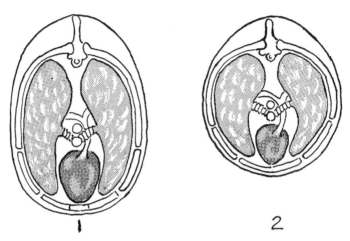

Heart and lung room is secured more by depth of body than width, so again the long, flat but well sprung rib gets a call over the round rib. A comparison between the sketches 1 and 2 shows what would have happened to the flat-ribbed dog's heart and lung room had nature given him barrel ribs even though they are as "well sprung."

The *herring gut* is likely caused by the shortness of the bony section of the ribs, forcing the sternum to reach up and meet them. However, the two seem to go hand-in-hand so old Jake chalked up another advantage with, "It was his two ribs that did it." The tremendous heart and lung space which the dog possessed enabled him to work right up to the end of those hot, exhaustive two hours without reducing his normal pace afield.

The actual length of the rib has more to do with heart

and lung capacity than its mid-curve. Certain breeds, such as the Bulldog, because of an effort to get a low center of gravity have sought the well-rounded-rib structure. In this, as in other things, give and take must be the guiding influence when a specific accomplishment necessitates a certain course. However, the fully rounded rib does not provide body depth in comparison to width as well as the flat mid section on the same rib. The deep, narrow body is more efficient for a field worker than the round. It provides better heart and lung room and aids in combatting lateral displacement in locomotion.

THE ABDOMINAL SECTION

The abdomen lies behind the rib section. It contains the stomach, liver and other intestines which are held in place by muscles attached to the last ribs, the front of the pelvis and the sides of the loin vertebrae, thus creating a cradle, so to speak. It is the purpose of the intestines to manufacture energy from food so that it can be transmitted to the various parts of the body by the transportation system of which the heart and lungs are the motor and clearing house.

There is a wide and powerful muscle extending from the tendons on the pelvis beneath this cradle to the base of the ribs and sternum. It draws the rib section backward, compresses the intestines, and is also the principal muscle that bends the spine. If the dog is *pot gutted,* this muscle is extended and unable to function correctly. When it does, it will push the pot gut into the diaphragm and interfere with its action. That is the reason that a pot gutted dog will come in from a short run "all out."

The functional value gained by a tuck-up is to get this muscle in a straight line where it will operate at its best during locomotion. In which case it should follow a straight line from the back tips of the pelvis to the sternum, the apparent curve being given it by the skin of the flank. As an aid to the intestine in expulsion, one of its major missions, it can do with a slight sag so that it produces action by going straight.

17

Dentition

DENTITION is so definitely a part of our dog's life in the field, show ring or home that it must be considered in his physical make-up. Few phases of the dog are less appreciated and at the same time subjected to criticism than his dental condition. Many good dogs have been taken out of their rightful heritage by lack of care, treatment and understanding of his teeth.

The first consideration is the name and location of the teeth. The small teeth in the exact front of the mouth are the *incisors*. There are six of these in each jaw, the upper and lower. They are tearing teeth. Next we encounter the *canines*, the largest teeth in the mouth, which are primarily the swords of battle. Behind the canines, we find the *molars* or jaw teeth. Some fields divide the latter into premolars, which are used for cutting, and the molars, which are used for grinding. Whether you choose to divide them or not, they are masticators and grinders.

A dental formula of permanent teeth can be stated as follows:

$$2 \, (\mathrm{I} \, \frac{3}{3} \quad \mathrm{C} \, \frac{1}{1} \quad \mathrm{PM} \, \frac{4}{4} \quad \mathrm{M} \, \frac{2}{3}) = 42$$

The numbers within the brackets start from the center of the mouth and represent first the upper and then the lower teeth as indicated by the letter. This gives the total number of upper and lower teeth on one side of the mouth and, multiplied by 2, the total which should be in the mouth of a mature dog.

There is an old story about an Irish emigrant who wrote

in the space for his place of birth, "Ireland, except my teeth." So it is with dogs for they have baby or milk teeth and later on shed them to secure permanent teeth.

We can tabulate temporary teeth as to number and the normal time for them to erupt as follows:

Incisors, 6 upper, 6 lower, erupt between 19 and 28 days.
Canines, 2   "   , 2   "   ,   "   "   3 and   5 weeks.
1st Molars do not appear in temporary teeth.
2nd Molars, 2 upper, 2 lower, erupt 4 to 6 weeks.
3rd Molars, 2   "   , 2   "   ,   "   3 to 4 weeks.
4th Molars, 2   "   , 2   "   ,   "   3 to 6 weeks.
The 5th, 6th and 7th molars do not appear in temporary teeth.

When the pup is born the teeth are not visible though the outlines can be picked up. Large breeds cut their teeth faster than small ones. A Dane or St. Bernard may

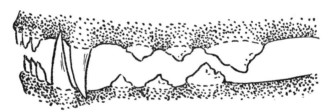

PUPPY TEETH. A complete set of puppy teeth as seen from side view. There are 3 incisors, 1 canine and 3 molars both top and bottom on each side.

have a complete set of milk teeth in the fourth week while small terriers and toys sometimes go to the sixth week. Female pups usually get their teeth before the male pups of the same litter. Summer puppies will finish the job much more quickly than winter pups of the same breeding.

Temporary teeth are rarely placed close together and as the pup grows the opening increases. The lower milk

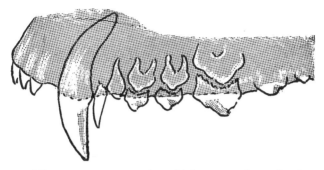

The permanent teeth, which come through the gums behind the puppy teeth, should push them out, for their roots have been reabsorbed by the system and probably become a part of the permanent teeth. Teeth that are not pushed out should be extracted.

teeth usually come through first but when permanent teeth appear it is likely the uppers which are first.

THE PERMANENT TEETH

The number of permanent teeth should be the same regardless of breed. However, it is not unusual to find missing dentition in any or all breeds. Some stud dogs cast down this mutation for mutation it is. Show-ring judges are often quite critical of this point while others pass on it only in close decisions. It is hereditary and therefore more serious than discolored teeth.

The number and eruption of permanent teeth are as follows:

Center incisors, 8, erupt 3 to 4 months.
Corner incisors, 4, " 5 to 6 months.
Canines, 4, " 4 to 6 months.
1st Molars, 4, " 4 to 5 months.
2nd Molars, 4, " 5 to 7 months.
3rd and 4th Molars, 8, usually follow 2nd.
5th Molars, 4, erupt 4 to 6 months.
6th Molars, 4, " 4 to 7 months.
7th Molars, 2, " 6 to 9 months.

The variation in time is due to breed and health or the animal's diet. The period of cutting permanent teeth is always critical; the mortality is higher at this time than any other age of the dog. This is probably due to the drain on the calcium and phosphorus supply in building

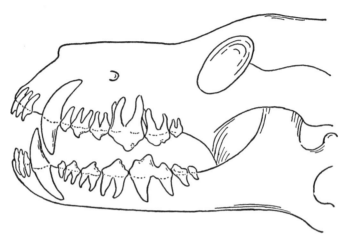

PERMANENT TEETH. The upper jaw contains 3 incisors, 1 canine and 6 molars on each side. The lower jaw has 3 incisors, 1 canine and 7 molars on each side. Quite often one or two of the front molars, top or bottom, will be missing in a mature dog.

the teeth and the bone which is being produced at the same time. There is strong evidence that we can increase susceptibility to distemper in dogs at this time by a deficiency in calcium and phosphorus and the vitamins which work with them.

The root of the temporary tooth, if things are normal, is reabsorbed into the pup's system leaving the tooth hanging as a shell at the gum lines. The permanent tooth then pushes it out.

It may happen that the same path of growth is not followed by the permanent tooth or that the root of the temporary tooth is not completely eroded away and re-

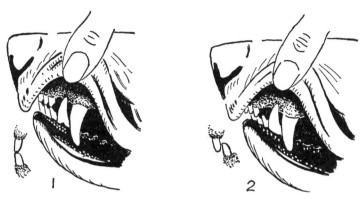

Level and Scissors Bite. Level Bite with the incisors strik-ing edge to edge. 2) Scissors Bite with the upper incisors striking just along the front face of the lower ones.

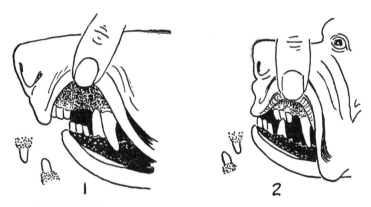

OVERSHOT AND UNDERSHOT. 1) An overshot jaw with the top incisors extended out beyond the lower ones. 2) An undershot jaw with the lower incisors extending be-yond the upper. As these are tearing teeth either of these jaw conditions is a fault where the dog's work would require such effort. In the Bulldog and some other breeds, tearing has not been required and they have sacrificed it to get the advantage of moving the power of the molars forward in the lower jaw as compared to the upper.

tains a grip firm enough to deflect the permanent tooth. This results in a double row of teeth. The canine quite often misses its milk counterpart but as it rarely deflects the permanent tooth it is not so serious.

Any temporary tooth which is causing deflection should be removed immediately. Aside from disfiguration of the teeth, the double row collects foreign matter that often causes irritations.

THE BITE

The majority of breed standards designate the type of *bite* desirable for the specific type of dog. This means the manner in which the teeth of the upper jaw meet those of the lower jaw.

In the *level bite* the incisors strike cutting edge to cutting edge. A *scissors bite* means that the upper incisors strike just forward of the lower, touching or barely missing them.

The *overshot jaw* finds the upper incisors striking some distance ahead of the lower, a condition that may not affect the teeth other than incisors. While this may be an abnormal extension of the upper jaw, it also can indicate the receding of the lower jaw.

The *undershot jaw* is the result of the lower jaw extending out in front of the upper. This is characteristic in many short faced breeds or those with *broken-up face* and is not a fault unless it interferes with the dog's natural work and living.

During the first few years of a dog's life its age wear can be judged fairly accurately by the condition of the incisors. This incisor has a center crown with two cusps or shoulders on each side. A dog fed the normal diet will show an average wear to the crown and cusps, relatively so anyway.

1 year—crown and both cusps are distinct.
2nd year—crown gradually disappears from lower centrals.
3rd year—middle incisors wear level.
4th year—cusps in upper centrals disappear.
5th year—the amount of incisor that is left is indication from here on.

However, the dog is particularly subject to tartar formations, which cause much of the discoloration on his teeth. This takes on a dirty brown color, starting at the gum line and being so smoothly applied that it may appear as the tooth itself until its surface is broken. Sometimes it will form in sharp, projecting edges that damage the tooth enamel. These formations should be chipped away by one experienced at the work.

The age of a dog can be judged fairly well in the first few years by the wear of the incisors. The crown first wears away to the cusps or shoulders and thence to the gums. Age indicated is approximately normal.

Diet with roughage which sets up friction wears away some of the tartar. It has not been our observation that "a bone a day, keeps tartar away"; bones do not reach the base of the tooth and often do considerable harm by excessive tooth wear. Hard biscuits will do a better cleaning job. Tough meat, gristle and skin are the natural teeth cleaners of the wild.

Tartar accumulation is not to be confused with enamel erosion. Age and bacteria will cause this erosion but mainly it is due to some devitalizing disease such as distemper. This is so universally true that almost any discolored tooth evokes the remark, "Distemper teeth." By the interference to metabolism, caused by high fever while the disease is in progress, the calcium deposits which make up the teeth do not form normally, the result being pitted and discolored teeth. This does not affect that part of the tooth that has come through the gum but that which is being formed below the gum line.

Distemper teeth are unsightly and judges often penalize them to a point tantamount to disqualification. However it has long been recognized by those in a position to observe that distemper teeth do not disintegrate any faster than clear teeth, often not as rapidly. Scar tissue is stronger than normal structure. These teeth have fought a battle and bear the honest scars of victory.

Dentition often gives us an insight into more than the dog's mouth for, as has been suggested, structural formation in one part of the dog indicates what might be expected in others. If the texture of the tooth is poor, we can expect to find the same condition in the calcium and phosphorus deposits in the skeleton bones. While this may not be true in all cases, it is a reasonable yardstick with which to measure this quality and the only visible one we have on the living dog.

18

Applying the Facts

UNLESS we can apply these facts to our personal experiences with dogs, whether in connection with judging or utilization, they are as useless as a toboggan in Havana. We get very little practical benefit from maxims collected as curios or pin-ups. Not unstrangely, it has been our desires and ideas that in many cases have upset the dog's balance and put his motility out of kilter. If we forget these and throw the dog on his own, in time he would solve or re-right his locomotive problems even as the animals of the wild have done. Some of the most perfectly moving canines found are street-running mongrels—they have to move right or they do not continue to run the streets.

You have no intention of forgetting your personal desires in these questions, hence the only answer is to rationalize locomotive factors to the determined purpose of your chosen breed. Let the Peke remain a pocket-size Chinese giant and the Dal sport his punctuation marks, but at the same time let us make good movers of them even though the movement does have some special characteristic.

Dogs have improved over their original pattern and this by the help of man. Perhaps greater strides were made during the last of the nineteenth and first of the twentieth centuries than during any other like period. Dogs were first bred to work more specifically and then standardized in type; the Dane ceased to be a boar or fanghound and became a Dane, the Setter and Pointer moved out from under your feet and cut western counties down to size, the Chihuahua turned around and walked under himself, and so on through practically every breed.

We realize that times have changed, more in the first half of the twentieth century than history had previously recorded. This change has taken our dogs out of the fields and off the roads and put them in backyards and living rooms, leaving the dictates of their characteristics almost wholly in the hands of fancy.

The changes wrought by fancy have improved the picture but not always the functional qualities of the products. Where for fact or fad, breeders chose to deviate from the natural rudiment, nature was often reluctant to make the change or, having made it, tossed in some other unexpected alteration.

Faults thus acquired were first tolerated and then accepted as one might wet feet on fishing trips. Eventually many ceased to be considered faults as breeders became accustomed to them. "Why, Collies are supposed to be cow-hocked," more than one breeder has informed us. "Gee, isn't he a beaut in the field!" the owner of a bench champion Setter exclaimed as blue belton fluff bobbed up and down a hundred feet ahead of us, trying to see over the next hill before making a run for it.

Applying the principles of functional locomotion and structure to individual breeds necessitates consideration of the basic intent. So we make no attempt to project them on each of the 100-odd existing breeds but, instead, to classify these breeds into working and social groups which meet relatively the same problems and indicate the important factors.

SPORTING DOGS

Sporting dogs work either feather or fur, and because of that they vary. Feather workers can be divided into three types: rangers, springers and retrievers. Based somewhat on training, we even have two types of rangers, the dogs which independently locate birds, freeze into point on them and hold until the huntsman arrives. A glimpse at field trials reveals this difference.

They are cutting a brace loose in an all-age stake; it's the Coming Storm and Homewood Flirtation, and both dogs streak toward a distant hedge-row, running straight and level. It would be impossible to follow them afoot, and throughout the day they will give a horse a good workout. They move around the hedge into the wind and cast out for nearly a half-mile to a cedar thicket, working at a rate of better than 15 miles an hour. They run straight, turned only by geography or signals from the handler. Though they can be slowed down and made to work close, they are at their best in wide, unrestricted country.

Later on, in a shooting dog stake, we watch Naillot of Aileach and Manitoba Pat. They move at a rate from two to three times as fast as their handlers walk, quartering the course from side to side in a zig-zag pattern. While the straight runner must have speed, endurance and a level gallop, the quartering dog does not need the speed but must move smoothly.

Restricted territory, whether urban or geographic, is ideal for "springer" hunting. These dogs are usually taken afield at heel and do not hunt for bird locations but are taken there by the huntsman. Once there they are sent ahead, remaining within gunshot range, to locate and spring the bird to wing.

These dogs, which are usually spaniels, do not need excessive speed. However, as they are smaller, the roughness of the ground is magnified and likewise their transportation problems. All feather workers can be taught to retrieve, but the springer is almost universally trained for this and the work must be taken into account when putting functional parts together on him.

To summarize them, they all need well-laid-back blades, long ribs, deep briskets, no indication of herring gut and a rear assembly that has as much drive as possible without over-matching the receiving ability of the front. Pasterns must have some slope and the feet should be of the type to match the speed required. We would say that it requires more care to produce the "straight" runner did we not fear the implication that the others could do top work if put together less efficiently.

Retrievers take us into the water as well as over land. On land, their physical requirements are relatively those of the "springer" or "quartering" dog but, in water, they meet entirely different problems which must be considered in their make-up. In addition to the breeds produced specifically for this work, a number of land spaniels are used, and we want to include the standard Poodle, for few dogs can do a better job on land or water.

It is an advantage to the swimmer for the center of gravity in the body to be moved back toward its center, taking weight off the forehand. This distributes the weight more evenly over the submerged area and the front feet do not have to fight so hard to keep the head afloat. The swimmer's main drive comes from the back legs; the front feet add very little to this but do keep the animal from doing a head dive. When the dog is carrying heavy game, this factor is still more important.

The center of gravity is moved backward by a relatively smaller head and shorter neck and a rearhand that is comparatively heavier than the forehand. The former is evident in the Labrador while the latter is found in the Chesapeake. Barrel ribs and breadth of body, rather than depth, are an aid to keeping the dog afloat but they are dangerous to play with lest we lose heart and lung room; these dogs need plenty of that, for it is no easy task to swim with an overbalancing weight which is ten per cent of the dog's body weight.

Ground speed is not essential, but the bones and muscles which propel the dog in swimming are the same as those which take him over the ground, and the principles of leverage and power used are also the same. So the general maxims established for speed can be applied to them.

SPORTING HOUNDS

Hounds are worked on fur and we find them divided into three general types: scent trailers, gaze trailers and the ones that go to ground. In each you have a number of variations. For instance, you will never see a single standard written that comprehensively covers the Foxhound. It may fit the pack hound, followed by horse, and be far wide of the upland night runner. A glance at the various requirements will make this understandable.

The star-splashed sky is little more than a slit overhead as mountain-sides fold in, while up and down over ragged rocks, along narrow ledges and through tightly laced azalea a wise old fox takes Mose Callahan's five slim-bodied, undersized Walkers for a race that would have lost a good pack hound within the first two miles. These dogs have to turn on acorns, walk mom's clothes line and run through the eye of a needle.

We turn from them to the Mid-west and eastern Rockies where in addition to fox, bob cat and mountain lion, they run the coyote and wolf for perhaps the toughest test given any dog. In the early evening the dogs break a wolf from the cover of a light woods and he takes out across the hills, talking back to them in no uncertain terms for a 10 to 15-hour race that defies the best horseman to follow. Try one of these dogs out some night; they will brush the cobwebs from your mind and you will understand why they cannot be duplicates of their more corky cousins running shoulder to shoulder in front of pink coats.

Then we have the slow, sure trailer. This one takes an old track and works it out until the game can be jumped and turned over to the faster dogs that run sometimes by scent and sometimes by gaze, depending on how close they are to the game. Even running by scent, it is as often brush scent rather than ground scent.

All types of Foxhounds, though, even the ones that serenade 'possums in persimmon trees, must put out a good smooth running job with agility, quick turning and sure-footedness in places, speed and endurance in others, or match strides with thoroughbred chasers and hunters over bars and fields.

The Beagles, singing to cottontails, run either in packs for the pleasure of their song or singly for the purpose of shooting game, have all the problems of locomotion to solve as do horses afield and this they do with a conformation not unlike that of a middle-weight hunter. The pack-running Beagle should not differ greatly from the strictly shooting dog, except in training and inclination to stay with the pack. The pack dog generally is not as fast and therefore he falls short at field trials and in the esteem of the huntsman.

There is a tendency in these dogs, particularly the small ones, to straight shoulders and pasterns; too often we see herring guts and bodies too wide for combatting lateral displacement. In this breed, as in many others, the dog with "show qualities" is often out of favor at field trials and with the men who hunt. "It's not how they look but how they run," is a common statement at field trials and one which could be corrected by giving them show dogs with proper moving equipment.

The Basset family, of which the Dachshund was once a variety, still offers an assortment of size and type of front leg. They are not ground coverers despite the fact that in France, where they are more popular than elsewhere, they are coursed in packs on the hare. They do make excellent underground dogs on the larger varmints.

The Basset is the largest of the little-big dogs, a 12-inch Basset often weighing above 40 pounds. High, powerful hindquarters with low withers brings him close to the ground in front. He has a forearm that is curved in various degrees with the out-turned pad.

This forearm curves inward as though seeking static balance and then, as it were, changes its mind at the pastern and the feet go out. They are broad, flat feet with large webs and often appear to be splayed. There is something to be said for this type front leg and foot for the animal that goes to ground—the mole does the world's best job of digging with a similar front leg and foot.

The Dachshund, originally a Basset, began toward the end of the nineteenth century to take on characteristics of the terrier and soon divided into two types: hound and terrier. The latter, with us today, is our best underground hound. Long, low-set with enough of the hound left for trailing and enough of the terrier to put fire into his work.

His body is slung down between his front legs which forces certain compromises in functional structure. We have pointed out the faults that accrue to these fronts if they are not carefully watched. The main one is an upright shoulder blade that slips around on the thoracic structure and gives leg action on a bias to the line of travel. Mechanically a slight inward curve of the forearm is an advantage to transverse balance and travel, provided the pastern does not turn out and the shoulder blade moves on a line with travel.

THE GAZEHOUNDS

The father of all gazehounds is the Greyhound whose origin is lost in antiquity. Down through his history, he was venerated by the Egyptians and coursed by Caesar. The Persians dressed them into the Afghan and Saluki, the Russians into the Borzoi, the Irish and Scotch put a wire coat on them for their Wolfhound and Deerhound, while the English cut the feed bill on their racing dogs with the Whippet.

Throughout the world there are several varieties of

A typical Greyhound bred and hunted for generations by the Bushmen over the heavy sands of the hot, trackless desert. They are extremely deep of brisket with plenty of heart and lung room.

Greyhounds, all used for their speed in running down game. They bear a family relation and some are quite good. In fact a study of them will show how work afield develops qualities of movement even when the dogs are bred by aborigines such as the Bushmen of the deserts who hunt jackals and other fleet game. Their Greyhounds, and every family has them, are rather uniformly good movers. The ones which the Englishman and American have developed, based on coursing and racing, are likely the most efficient.

There is a Sunday crowd boxing off the street of a little Lancashire town; it is tensely quiet, straining on tip-toes to see over shoulders. Then suddenly it bursts into one wild, unintelligible roar. Five little, slim-bodied dogs race down the center of the road; a brindle in the lead but a fawn closing fast from the rear. Almost quicker than the eye they are past and in the arms of their owners—and another collier's family will eat next week.

These coal miners liked a sport with competition and were gamblers under their grime even as the Ladies of London town under their silks. They had not the money to own horses nor even the space to race Greyhounds so they developed the Whippet, the world's smallest bang-tail. It was not unusual for them to bet an entire week's pay on the Sunday races so the welfare of the women and children depended more on the quality of their dogs than the father's ability to dig coal.

Whippet racing has been almost as popular in Maryland ever since Felix Leser first introduced it to the Valley. Informal Sunday races are punctuated with rye highballs and summer evenings are spent at the club where they have an oval track. There, it is more for pleasure than profit, for in Maryland it is still a sin to bet on anything that doesn't eat oats. These Whippets, however, are the poor man's race horse.

The value of dog or thing to the human race can properly be based on the number of people who derive pleasure or benefit from it. From that angle, the Greyhound stacks up as the world's most valuable canine breed. Even a small-time track, where betting is legal, will in 45 days of racing entertain more than 60,000 patrons and have better than two million dollars go through its mutuals. The relative attendance is based on the quality of dogs running—they must be good or the attendance isn't. Aside from racing, thousands of these dogs are coursed on natural game or run at regulated coursing trials, where again the dog must be built right to win.

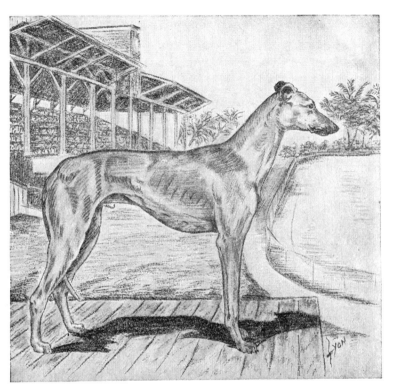

A typical Greyhound stake winner on the Florida dog tracks. As a class they are faster than any Greyhounds bred in other parts of the world, except England, at distances of three furlongs or less.

It does take something more than body conformation to out-course a jack-rabbit, sprinting at 40 miles per hour, or get under the wire ahead of other dogs on the track; it takes the will to get out and do it. It is also a safe bet that the one which does it consistently is built right for the job and is just as pleasing to the eye for that fact.

All the general factors of speed which we have discussed apply to these dogs with special emphasis on some. For one thing, their fronts must be particularly good for, in addition to its regular work, it must propel the dog into a second period of suspension in each sequence.

There is no exaggerated arch to the good runner's back lines; the back itself is flat and the loin has a key-stone arch. The body is narrow, flat-sided and extremely deep in the chest with no indication of herring gut. The tuck-up should not deprive the dog of sufficient intestinal space but be rather an illusion caused by the extreme depth of the chest. The long upper arm is essential; the straight terrier front often seen on Whippets is not. Pasterns can slope as much as is practical without indicating a lack of muscular strength to straighten them, for they must be straightened to get driving power.

The well bent stifle is necessitated by a long upper and lower thigh to get muscular length and action from these two members. The hock joint itself must be broad with a long os calsis; close to the ground for endurance, set high for initial speed. Feet must have thick heel pads, long third digits with upright second digits.

The dog should move "high-footed," showing ability to flex all four legs. Muscles should be well developed without being bunchy and knotty; this applies especially to the rearing muscles and those which flex pasterns and toes. Although these comments seem to be directed at the Greyhound, we are thinking equally of the Saluki, Afghan and Borzoi.

THE TERRIERS

Terriers took their name either from the Latin *terra,* meaning earth, or the French *terrier,* meaning the hole of the rabbit. Therefore they must have been intended solely for going to ground despite the fact that some varieties have been developed which are too large for anything but surface work. For this discussion, we shall consider them as underground workers.

The major characteristics for both high and low center of gravity types were pointed out in the discussion of special fronts. Elbow action must be above the brisket line. The threatening fault of the straight shoulder blade should never be tolerated, particularly if it has moved up on the neck or around the chest wall on a bias to the travel line.

Neither type of the fronts on terriers is designed for speed and long reach, therefore care must be observed in putting power in the rear assembly lest the dog be forced to pound or pad. The latter may look good in the show ring because it is high stepping and fancy but it is not conducive to steady movement.

All terriers need relatively long heads to get the bite out in defense of the digging pads when meeting the varmint. Incisors and canines are more important to a terrier's initial bite than the molars.

One thing which must be watched in long headed dogs is the natural tendency for other members of the body to lengthen in ratio to head over a series of generations to give natural balance. This will put the dog high on the leg, not covering enough ground.

WORKING DOGS

The very expression *working dog* indicates the necessity for good movement whether in draft, mountain climbing, herding stock, home guarding, barn hustling or police and army service.

Tooling a 60-foot string of dogs and sledge over the frozen snow between trees that nature planted too carelessly, or through village traffic operating even more carelessly requires a little more than the call of "ouk" and "radder" or "har." These dogs must be built for pulling even as those are in the shafts of Belgian milk carts.

For speed, we take a blend between the conformation of the draft horse and that of a strong running Pointer or other unimpeded worker. We must have shoulders and fronts that will take the push generated in the back assembly, enough weight to be thrown into the collar effectively, large nostrils and windpipe, deep bodies, relatively narrow fronts, slightly sloping pasterns and cat-feet.

Sledge dogs need not be limited to Eskimos, Samoyedes, Huskies and Malamutes—any good strong dog can be hooked to a sledge for a thrill you will never forget—but to do the work properly they must be built for draft, whether fast or heavy.

In the larger working dogs such as Danes, Pyrenees, St. Bernards, Newfoundlands and Mastiffs, feet and legs are of utmost importance. Some of these breeds have accumulated faults in this respect which prohibit effective movement and which many breeders seem to take for granted as they do ears and tails.

A half-flight down old Roxy hammered at a heel lift and waxed philosophical over the passing feet that could be seen through the narrow window.

" 'Tain't shoes you see—it's people. There goes the cigar girl at the drug store." He pointed his hammer at a trim pair of ankles. "She was out late last night and don't feel so chipper. And there's Mr. Brown from the bank. Don't ask him for a loan today—he played golf yesterday and his arches are hurting. Yeah, you're looking at people if you just study how to read 'em."

We have thought of that often as we watched the big dogs judged. They seem more resigned to bad feet though than their owners, at least they do not become as grouchy. These big dogs have a lot to carry and bad feet should never be condoned in them.

Were we to purchase one of these dogs, we would start

judging him at the feet and go from there up the legs. If the pastern is straight, it will soon start knuckling over; with too much slope, age and work will break it down. The cow-hocked dog and the heifer in your pasture will move very much alike.

Another prevalent characteristic in big dogs, also in draft horses, is that the back leg flexes only slightly when moved forward; it seems to swing like a pendulum from the hip joint. Often you can hear the pads or nails scraping the floor as they are shuffled forward. Again you notice that the croup is pitched into the air by the straightening of the back leg to give this pendulum swing clearance. This is wasted motion and energy for it is not along the line of travel.

Perhaps you should not expect these dogs to flex the back leg as much as a Pointer or Shepherd but you would like to feel that they can step over a rock in the field without stubbing their toes. We kept one once for a friend but soon had to stop letting him run the open fields with our own dogs; the tops of his back feet became too severely scratched by dewberry briars.

The middle-weight working dogs, such as the Collie, Boxer, Belgian and Old English Sheepdog differ somewhat in gait from the Doberman and German Shepherd.

The Doberman works at a canter, when cruising, and often uses the double suspension gallop like that of gazehounds when he puts on speed. Therefore his conformation should be somewhat of a blend. This gait combination is excellent for his work; in the canter he has endurance, and the double suspension gallop provides speed to terminate quickly any accomplishment.

The German Shepherd is the only dog being bred specifically with the suspension trot as a working gait. This is known in horses as the *flying trot,* and is subject to all the conditions that necessitate putting boots on horses. The stride is long and the leg is exceedingly well flexed in action. Long couplings do not add to speed but often are too weak to bridge the distance between front and rear assemblies. However, this dog must be long coupled for you cannot boot a dog or prevent the short-coupled ones from crabbing unless they are also short in gait.

The Shepherd, though, is not actually long in body but rather slightly short of leg, bringing him closer to the ground, making him "cover more ground" in ratio to his height.

The flying trot lowers the traveling level of the center of gravity quite markedly from the standing level because the legs are flexed more than in the normal trot. When the gait goes off with speed, there is an obvious drop to the back line which should maintain that level with a smoothness almost capable of carrying a glass of water on it. As the acute angulation of his back legs necessitates standing and moving slowly with a sickle hock, the question arises as to whether or not the individual can straighten this joint. If not, it is a decided fault.

Take away from this dog either the well-laid-back shoulder, long upper arm, the body length ratio, acute angulation of the back leg or ability to flex and extend both front and back legs to a high degree, and you will not have the flying trot. Without that, this is just another trotting dog.

The herdsmen gave us several varieties of dogs, all of which should remain capable of working wherever cattle and sheep roam. They should have sufficient speed to turn back the occasional stray and be sure of foot in any kind of going. Ability to turn quickly and initial spring are desirable qualities. Slightly steeper croups and well-let-down hocks are an advantage, as is the sickle hock if it will straighten in action. But cow hocks are a decided hindrance even though the cows being herded do have them.

Shelties should be particularly adapted to working over rough ground.

The Corgi is another small worker intended to bump cattle about the barn and keep down rodents. He is built on the lines of a terrier with low center of gravity so he can work into small places about the barn. What has been said about other low dogs applies to this one.

THE TOYS

Small dogs, particularly those classed as toys, are too often considered for two qualities only: either head and size, or coat and size. Perhaps we should say lack of size. But these little animals are still dogs and proportionately have all the transportation and living requirements of others.

Breeding ultra-miniatures would not be difficult if every part of the dog went down uniformly and maintained the same relation to other parts. Nature will not play ball with us like that. For one thing, eyes will not reduce as fast as the skull and we soon have eyes setting out in front of the skull instead of deep in protective sockets.

Nature and injudicious selection of breeding stock scrambles the picture in other ways when the animal goes too small. The limit to size should not be on poundage but the maximum reduction where the dog still retains well placed shoulders, set back on the side of the ribs rather than up on the neck, good legs and particularly feet that do not resemble little talons.

Unless you seek a low center of gravity as in the Peke, sound function cannot be had with a long coupling, so body length should not exceed withers' height. Long bodies tend to be round with lack of depth, and they do not provide sufficient strength to span the gap between front and rear assemblies. Often these bodies appear long because the shoulders are too much advanced on them.

Unless feet have gone down proportionately in size, the muscles activating the toes lack the strength to keep the foot compact.

Shoulder placement on the Pekingese will have to re-

Obedience exercises will be the extent of work demanded of the average dog. They are much easier for the dog that is built to move correctly and by the same token more satisfaction to the owner.

main "around front" slightly to bring shoulder points closer together than the elbows when they are tight against the body. It is this placement that accounts for the characteristic roll of the Peke, which should be a roll and not a waddle.

Remember that all these little fellows must move and have sufficient room for the factory equipment that keeps them alive. The toy that races across a 20-foot room has run proportionately as far as a Shepherd crossing a 60-foot lawn. When the toy jumps from your lap to the floor he has received an equal shock to the average obedience trial dog scaling a 6-foot fence. If you keep these facts in mind as you minimize these dogs, you will appreciate their need of functional conformation.

The vast majority of our dogs are personal companions and we have a number of breeds which as a whole fall into that category. They are all covered by the four types of body structure which have been discussed: low center of gravity, terrier fronts, the normal and the double suspension galloper.

The working test of companion dogs likely reaches its maximum in obedience classes and local clubs promoting these exercises, plus romps about the home. Obedience clubs can do more than any other agent to convert dog owners to the desire for dogs which are functionally sound. We have never seen a non-golfer converted to the game by watching tournament matches, but we have seen the occasional park player develop into tournament material because of association with better golfers and the pride in achievement thus stimulated. So association with better dogs under working conditions will likewise stimulate an owner's desire for better dogs which can move and work more efficiently.

We have said that we take no issue with the way standards are written. As a final thought, we modify that for we do take issue with the way many are interpreted. Because of that we have stressed the work of the dog in the field, in competitive trials and on the race track even though we know that the majority of dogs will not compete in these fields. In one salient respect, dogs are no different than any other sport or hobby. We, as individuals, will get out of them no more than we put into them. If we like dogs for the sake of owning them or the pleasure of using them, we should want the individual to have the requisites of a functionally sound animal.

We cannot approach overall perfection by stressing a few characteristic features such as size, coat, expression of head, the color of eyes or the set of ears if we let these submerge functional conformation or any part of it. Do not breed just a dark eye or a button ear; first breed a sound dog and then go for the dark eye and the button ear. Put functional soundness above everything else whether the dog goes afield or spends his life curled in your lap, and he will get more out of life and you will get more out of him.

Glossary

Achilles tendon. A combination of tendon and muscle (gastrocnemius) extending from the femur along the back of the gaskin or lower thigh to the os calcis which is the major hock bone; its function is to straighten the hock and deliver power to the stride of the back leg.

angulation. The angles formed by the lines and planes of the various parts of the dog's body with themselves and the ground; specifically applied to the front and back leg assemblies.

articulation. The joining or juncture of bones and the movement of one on the other at the junctures.

back. That part of the back line composed of the five vertebrae between the withers and the loin; the 9th to 13th vertebrae inclusive. Often loosely or incorrectly used to include other parts of the back line.

back line. The top line or profile of the dog from neck to base of tail, including withers, back, loin and croup.

ball and socket. Joints that have a ball or knob articulating in a socket.

barrel. The rib section or thorax of a dog when it is approximately cylindrical in form.

barrel ribs. Ribs that follow a circular line of relatively the same degree from spinal column to juncture with brisket.

base of support. The foundation created under the dog by the supporting legs. The static or stationary base is set up by the 4 legs when the dog is not in motion. The kinetic or moving base is prescribed by the number and position of legs supporting body weight in the gait.

bat ear. Erect ears that suggest a round tip resembling those of the bat; characteristic of the French Bulldog.

blade. The shoulder blade or scapula.

bone. A chemical formation of solidified animal and mineral matter that is a unit of the dog's skeleton. The word when used as an expressive term, usually in conjunction with *well, up* or *light of,* indicates the relative size of the general collection of bones in the skeleton.

brisket. The heavy cartilage and bone formation at the base of the thorax or rib section to which the ribs find ultimate attachment; sternum, breastbone. In conjunction with *deep of* or *shallow of* it indicates relative depth of the thorax.

brush. A long-coated and full tail as on the fox or the Collie.

bull neck. A neck heavy and short by comparison with other parts of the dog; a fault in some breeds, necessary to the type in others.

button ear. An ear held partly erect and close to the skull with the upper half folding over and tips pointing to the outside corners of the eye.

calf-knee. Said of a horse's knee, which is normally straight, that inclines backward with a slope from knee to pastern, metacarpal or shank, as is characteristic of a calf. Any dog with a sloping pastern is, by the same consideration, calf-kneed.

canines. The two upper and two lower fang-like teeth just back of the incisors.

cannon bone. The section between hock joint and foot of the back leg; the metatarsal bones.

canter. A designating name for the sustained gallop. A three-time gait made up of a rear, a diagonal and a front support; it becomes the normal gallop when the diagonal splits making it a four-time gait.

camel back. A convex curved back line from neck to croup.

carpals. A cluster of small bones forming the pastern joint and of which the pisiform, an L-shaped bone, is the most important to locomotion.

cartilage. A tough, slightly flexible tissue somewhat like and often functioning as a bone; it forms the capping or bearing surface at joints; gristle.

cat-foot. A deep, round, compact foot which is characterized by a short third digit bringing the toes nearer the base or heel pad, resembling a cat's paw.

center of gravity. That point in a dog's body upon which all acting forces are equal; if the dog could be suspended on it, he would be in perfect balance. It is located on the horizontal center line, near the back edge of the forehand and not in the center of the dog's body. Also it is the point in the front, rear or other assembly of bones when opposing forces are equal.

cerebellum. The middle of the three parts of the brain; it reacts to reflexes, coordinates muscular action and is possibly the seat of natural instincts.

cerebrum. The first of three brain sections, located just behind the eyes; has to do with intellect and the ability to rationalize.

chest. The front area of the dog's body at the terminus of the sternum or breast bone.

clipping. The striking of the front legs by the back feet when the dog gaits. To avoid this the dog usually crabs or runs with his body at an angle to the line of progress.

conformation. The degree with which the various angles and parts of the dog agree or conform with one another and the general purpose or pattern demanded of the individual breed.

cocygeal vertebrae. The vertebrae of the tail; five to 22 depending on the breed.

covering ground. The amount of ground covered by the spread between front and back normal supports when compared to the height from ground to the brisket; strictly a question of ratio between these measurements and relatively the same as *daylight under the dog.*

coupling. That part of the body between and coupling the forehand to the rearhand, not to be confused with body length.

cow-hocks. Hocks pointing inward toward one another and out of a straight line from hip to paw; typical of cows.

crabbing. The act of a dog moving side-wise or crab-like with its body at an angle to the line of progress. The back feet thus step past the front feet without clipping them.

crank tail. A short, bent tail resulting from mutation.

croup. That part of the back line above the pelvis, from the loin section to the after end of the body.

daylight under the dog. An expression referring to the height from ground to brisket when compared to the distance between front and rear supports of the body; strictly a ratio between the distances and relatively the same as *covering ground.*

dentition. The process of growth or cutting of teeth and their arrangement in the dog's mouth.

dew claws. Extra claws or rudimentary toes, single or double, on the inside of the back legs and above the feet. This growth would have been the big toe on a five-toed foot but has mutated to the present status. A similar growth shows on the inside of the front leg which would have been the thumb in a five-fingered hand. They are demanded on some breeds; not present or removed on others to avoid injury.

diagonals. The support of the body in movement by legs located diagonally from one another such as the right front and left rear.

diaphragm. A large muscular tissue separating the thorax or rib section from the abdomen, completely bisecting the body and functioning in the breathing action.

digits. The first, second and third bones beginning at the nail of the dog's foot; the third bone forming the bridge of the foot, the first two its front supports.

distemper teeth. Teeth that have become discolored and sometimes pitted during the fever period of distemper or other sickness; only that portion of the tooth which has not passed the gum line is affected.

dock tail. A tail with a portion removed at some given vertebrae; cut or docked tail.

down in pasterns. Showing an angle forward or to the side which is abnormal; sometimes faulty bone assembly but usually due to weakness of the supporting tendons and muscles.

dorsal vertebrae. The thirteen vertebrae to which the ribs are attached; they form the withers and back.

draught dogs. Numerous breeds which are used to draught loads such as the sledge dogs or those drawing carts in Belgium and Holland; draft dogs.

dynamics. The science which investigates the action of force; static balance deals with forces at rest, kinetic balance with forces in motion.

elbow. The joint between the upper arm (humerus) and the forearm (radius and ulna); the point of elbow being the tip of the ulna or the outer portion of the curve of this joint.

elbows out. Elbows turning out from the body or normal line established by the breed's pattern; sometimes not manifest until the dog gaits. *Out at elbows. Moving out at elbows.*

ewe neck. A concave top line of neck resembling the neck of the ewe or camel.

extensors. Any muscle that straightens or extends a limb.

femur. The bone of the thigh, between the pelvis and stifle joint.

fibula. The smaller of two bones in the gaskin or second thigh; it functions primarily as a transmitter of leverage but is often fused at the base with the tibia in old animals.

fiddle front. A combination of out at the elbows, pasterns close together and turned out feet; usually with curved forearm.

field trial. A regulated competition in trained canine skill, particularly in locating and handling furred and feathered small game afield; may also be applied to the exercises of obedience and service work competition.

flat croup. A croup with less downward inflection from the back line than is deemed suitable to the pattern of the breed in question; usually with less than 30-degree slope to the ground.

flat sided. Said of a dog whose ribs are relatively flat in their midsection; particularly from the fifth rib backward.

flexors. Any muscle that bends or flexes a limb.

floating rib. The last or 13th rib which extends back into the area below the loin; usually unattached to the adjacent rib as are the ends of the other ribs, thus deriving its name.

forearm. The section of the front leg between the elbow and the pastern joint which is composed of the radius and ulna.

fore face. That part of the head in front of the eyes; muzzle.

forehand. The combined assemblies of the two front legs and the body which comes directly between them as we divide the dog into three sections: forehand, coupling, rearhand.

gait. Any one of the various types of coordinated leg actions when the dog is moving; movement in the proper or designated manner.

gallop. A term applying to three types of gait: the sustained or canter, the normal gallop and the leaping style or double suspension gallop.

gaskin. That part of the hind leg of a quadruped between the stifle and hock joints, embracing the tibia and fibula. Habitually used in the paddock though the dog fancy usually refers to this section of the leg as the second or lower thigh.

gay tail. A tail carried above the back line and flying flag-like; usually very active in vibrations.

gazehound. Any one of the various hound breeds that run or course game by sight rather than scent.

goose-rump. A croup that is steeper than prescribed by the pattern of the breed in question; any exceptionally steep croup, usually sloping more than 30 degrees to the ground.

go-to-ground. The act of the dog going or being sent into the ground to dig out or pursue game which has taken refuge either from trailing hounds or pursuit, usually into holes or natural burrows.

great dorsal muscle. A triangular sheet of muscle starting over the loin and the last four dorsal vertebrae, thence wrapping around and attaching to the ribs and terminating in a tendon which is inserted on the head of the humerus. It has many functions among which are rotating the ribs, drawing the front leg backward and being a part of the rearing muscles.

hare-foot. A deep, compact, oval or elongated foot, characterized by long third digits which extend the toes out from the heel pad to give greater leverage. It is not to be confused with a broken down cat-foot. A typical specimen is found on the rabbit or hare, hence its name.

height of the dog. The distance from the ground to the top of the withers. A standard measuring stick, with a sliding arm, is used to determine this in bench shows.

herring gut. An upsweep to the bottom profile line of the thorax from between or near the front legs to the abdomen or loin section which reduces the depth of the thorax and takes away heart room.

hip joint. The ball and socket joint between thigh and pelvis.

hock. The assembly of tarsus bones in the back leg which make the joint at the lower end of the second thigh or gaskin and the cannon bone or metatarsal bones.

hocks-well-let-down. A term which is synonymous with *hocks close to the ground;* this produces a relatively short distance between the hock joint and the ground, a short cannon bone, which reduces the leverage tax on the Achilles tendon and lessens fatigue.

hocky. Faulty hocks.

humerus. The bone of the upper arm, between shoulder blade and elbow.

incisors. The six upper and six lower front teeth, situated between the upper and lower canine teeth.

in-shouldered. Blades set too close at the joint between them and upper arms; usually found on those which are too upright and which are set on the front of the thorax rather than on its side walls.

jaws. The upper and lower part of the foreface, the bones of which carry the teeth.

kinetic balance. The state of forces being in balance when in motion; angulation and conformation that give balance to the dog when he is moving. It is a phase of dynamic balance.

knee. The stifle joint in the back leg which is quite similar to the human knee with its cap. Occasionally used to mean the pastern of the dog which is like the horse's knee.

knuckling-over. Bending forward or vibration of the pastern joint from the vertical line of support in the front leg; characteristic of straight pasterns and pronounced in physical weakness or old age.

lastissimus dorsi. A muscle described as the great dorsal.

lateral displacement. The force set up by the center of gravity moving from right to left and back when the dog is in motion, due to power being applied alternately on opposite sides of the body and the fact that the center of gravity is located in the front half rather than center of the body.

laws of leverage. In mechanics or physics any bar or prod capable or turning or moving on a fixed point, called the fulcrum (F), and having two counteracting forces, such as power (P) and weight (W), acting at other points and setting up mechanical ratios, is subject to the position and order of the three factors: PFW, PWF, and WPF.

lay-back of ribs. The angle which the ribs incline backward from the spinal column to the segment of the curve that changes their course forward to the juncture with the brisket.

laid-back shoulder. A shoulder blade inclined backward from the joint to the top at an efficient angle for the dog's work or action; 45 degrees being the most efficient angle.

leading leg. In the canter it is the leg which is not a part of the diagonal and which bears weight longer than the other front leg; the last acting front leg in the sequence. In the other gallops it is also the last acting front leg in the sequence and its straightening produces suspension.

leaping style gallop. A four-time gait with two periods of suspension, one following the straightening of the leading front leg and the other that of the opposite back leg; characteristic of gazehound, antelope and cheetah.

leggy. Legs too long for the rest of the dog, producing too much daylight under it and not covering enough ground.

level bite. The upper and lower front teeth (incisors) striking in line or edge to edge.

level gait. A gait in which there is little or no rise and fall to the withers due to the action of the center of gravity in the dog's body.

loaded shoulders. Shoulder blades under which the muscles, particularly those supporting the top half, have been developed so that the top of the blade is pushed outward from the body and cannot occupy its natural position.

loin. The section between the ribs and the croup; seven lumbar vertebrae.

long dorsal muscle. A muscle extending on both sides of the top of the spinal column from pelvis to neck and attached to all vertebrae between, flexing and extending the entire column; the two sides may coordinate or act independently.

longissimus dorsi. A muscle described as the long dorsal.

lumbar vertebrae. The seven vertebrae of the loin section between the dorsal and sacral vertebrae; they have longer transverse spires than other vertebrae.

low center of gravity front. A forehand in which the body has been let down closer to the ground between front leg assemblies in which the length rather than actual size of all bones has been reduced without affecting dynamic balance. The Scottie and Dachshund are examples.

measurements. Body length is taken from the forward point of the brisket to the after tip of the pelvis; height from the top of withers to the ground; body depth is taken from the back to the underline at the base of the eighth rib. Measurements of individual parts such as gaskin, cannon bone or let down of hocks must be considered in ratio with adjacent or other parts.

medulla. One of three parts of the brain; controls breathing and connects the other two parts to the spinal cord.

metacarpus. The bones from pastern joint to foot of the dog's front leg; the shank or metacarpal bones.

metatarsus. The bones between the hock joint and back foot of the dog; the cannon bone or metatarsal bones.

milk teeth. The temporary or puppy teeth.

molars. Twelve upper and fourteen lower back teeth in the dog's mouth; only six upper and six lower being present in temporary teeth.

momentum arc. The arc over which the center of gravity travels when lifted and then carried forward by momentum.

muscle. A contractile tissue made up of a fleshy center section and terminating in tendons which attach it to the framework of the dog. The fleshy part derives strength from cross section area and action by being able to contract two-thirds its length.

muscle tone. The quality or health condition of muscle tissue. The health or reflexive snap of the tissues binding the skin to the body gives a fair indication of muscle tone.

navicular. A small bone formed between the cartilage and tendons behind the juncture of the first and second digits; it acts as a ball bearing to the tendon and helps to keep the digits in relative placement.

neck. The first seven vertebrae (cervical) of the spinal column from head to withers; the number is the same in all dogs.

oblique shoulders. Shoulder blades sloping back at an efficient angle for the action and work of the dog, 45 degrees being the most efficient.

occiput. The high point of and at the back edge of the skull; occipital protuberance.

os calcis. A long bone in the tarsus assembly or hock joint, the tip forms the knob at the back side of the joint; it provides the lever for the action of the Achilles tendon on the joint, the cannon bone and foot.

out-at-elbows. Elbows protruding from the body or natural line from shoulder joint to foot when viewed from the front; may show only in movement.

out-at-shoulders. Blade set that places the joints too wide apart for efficient movement or balance; the opposite of in-shouldered (q.v.).

overshot. The incisors of the upper jaw striking in advance and not touching those of the lower jaw; degree depends on the advance.

padding. Picking the front feet higher than normally would be necessary in the forward stride while gaiting.

pads. The tough or callus formation on the bottom of the toes and heel of the dog's foot; the soles of the foot.

pace. A two-time gait made up of laterals only; the right front and rear followed by left front and rear; the amble.

pastern. The assembly of small bones at the juncture of forearm (radius and ulna) with the metatarsals or shank bones; sometimes used to designate all bones between forearm and foot.

patella. A cap-like bone composed mostly of cartilage at the stifle joint; it is like and functions the same as the human knee cap.

pectoral muscle. The muscle beneath and on both sides of the rib structure, attached to the ribs and inserted on the heads of the humerus bones, acting to draw the upper arms backward.

pelvis. A cage-like set of bones attached to the after end of the spinal column; providing the foundation for the back legs and activating muscles.

pigeon-toed. Feet, not necessarily the legs, inclined inward toward one another and placed or acting at an angle to the line of progress.

pile. Thick, heavy coat as seen on the Collie.

pisiform. An L-shaped bone in the carpal assembly or pastern joint; it supplies the leverage for the action of this joint and the bones below it; its tip shows as a knob at the back of the joint.

plume. A long-coated tail carried like a plume.

pole. The juncture of the second and third cervical vertebrae in the neck; sometimes showing a marked change in the convex curve of the neck's top line.

pot gutted. A distended abdomen from excess contents, slacking or sagging of supporting muscles.

pounding. The front feet striking the ground before the arc of momentum has expended itself and receiving the shock of both gravity and momentum.

psoas magnus. A muscular band beneath the spinal column acting as a balance to the long dorsal in flexing and extending the column; the tenderloin section of a steak when cut from a cow.

quality. That added touch to conformation, expression and character which marks the difference between competitive animals when they are projected against one another or the desired pattern of their breed.

radius bone. The front and weight bearing bone of the forearm.

rearhand. The combined assemblies of the back legs and croup; one of the three divisions of the dog's body: forehand, coupling and rearhand.

rearing muscles. The combination of the muscles that straighten the back legs with those of the loin and body which act when the entire body weight is on one or both back legs; they are all utilized in putting drive to the back leg.

rhomboideus. One of the shoulder muscles.

ribbed-up. Long ribs angling backward approximately 45 degrees in the first part of their travel from spinal column to brisket;

the phrase is usually emphasized by the adjective *well*. The length and angle of the last or floating rib indicates these features in the others.

ring tail. A tail curled over the back.

roach-back. Excessive convex curve of back line from the eighth rib to and sometimes over the croup; may show only as an excess in the loin section.

rocking horse. A dog that moves with too much rise and fall to the withers; bobbing across the field like a rocking horse.

rose ear. The ear that folds down and back exposing the inside burrs as seen on Bulldog and Greyhound.

saber tail. A tail carried low in semi-circle; example, German Shepherd.

sacral vertebrae. Three vertebrae, fused together, following the loin vertebrae; provide attachment for the pelvis.

sacrum. The croup or sacral vertebrae.

scapula. The shoulder blade; flat and somewhat triangular with a ridge approximately on its center line.

scissors bite. When the cutting edges of the upper incisors strike slightly in advance of those in the lower jaw, passing them but with faces still touching as do the blades of scissors; other teeth not affected.

screw tail. A product of mutation that is kinky and knotty.

second thigh. The section of back leg between stifle joint and hock; gaskin.

sequence. The coordinated result of a single stride of all four legs in any gait.

serratus. A muscle, described in shoulder muscles.

sesamoid. A small bone formed between the cartilage and tendons behind the juncture of the third digit and metacarpal or metatarsal bone; acts as a ball bearing for tendons and a chock to keep the involved bones in place.

shallow barred. Lack of desired depth in the rib section.

shallow brisket. Lack of depth in the rib section.

shelly. Narrow body, little spring to ribs; basically the latter.

short body. The total length of body being short when compared to coupling or the dog's height; dependent on general pattern of the breed.

short coupled. Short and compact between fore and rearhand.

shoulder. The region created by the shoulder blade and supporting muscles.

shoulder muscles. The group of muscles supporting and activating the shoulder blade. The main ones of the top half are the *rhomboideus,* a triangular muscle beneath the blade, and the *trapezius,* similar in shape, above the blade; they cushion the blade and rotate the tip. The lower half gets its main support from the serratus which extends back to the ribs and forward to the neck and suspensory ligament; it also acts to rotate the blade.

side-wheeler. A dog moving with body at an angle to the line of progress; crabbing (q.v.).

single tracking. When gaiting, the act of inclining the entire front and back leg inward so that the pads fall under, or nearly so, the vertical center of gravity in the body; the pad marks of all four feet approach a single center line.

sickle hocked. Standing with hock joint bent so that the cannon bone is at an angle rather than vertical to the ground creating a curve that suggests a sickle.

sickle tail. A tail carried high in a semi-circle.

slab-sided. Flat ribs with too little spring from spinal column.

slew-feet. The feet, not necessarily the legs, turned outward from the center line; sometimes termed *east and west.*

sloping shoulders. Oblique or angulated to a desired degree for efficient action; 45 degrees being the most efficient.

snipy face. A slender tapering face, lacking fill-in before the eyes and bone foundation above the teeth of the upper jaw.

spread hocks. Hocks pointing outward when standing or in motion; the opposite of cow-hocks. Back feet operate at an angle rather than parallel to the line of progress.

spinal column. A column of related bones (vertebrae) extending from the head to the tip of tail; it is the keel or foundation upon which the dog is built.

spinal cord. A group of nerves extending down the spinal column from the brain and lines branching off to individual sections of the body; the trunkline for coordination and communication of all parts behind the brain.

splay foot. A foot with toes spread wide apart; usually with flat toes and no arch.

squirrel tail. A tail curled over the back, midway between a sickle and ring tail.

standing-well-up-hocks. Standing with the cannon bone, between hock joint and paw, vertical to the ground when viewed from the side.

static balance. The balance of an assembly when it is not in motion; one of two phases of dynamic balance.

stern. The tail composed of five to 22 vertebrae.

sternum. The brisket or breast bone; the bottom outline of the thorax in profile extending upward to juncture with neck.

stifle joint. The joint between the upper and second thigh or gaskin in the back leg.

straight hocked. Lacking sufficient bend in the juncture of the second thigh or gaskin with the hock assembly or cannon bone.

straight pasterns. Pasterns with little or no slope to the bones between the joint and the foot.

straight shoulders. Shoulder blades not laid back to an efficient working angle with the ground.

stride. The distance from one pad mark to the next of the same foot in any gait.

suspension. The period when all legs are off the ground in the gait.

suspensory ligament. A large web-like ligament along the top of the neck, attached to its vertebrae and the first four dorsal vertebrae. It is divided into two parts; one a cord extending from the first two vertebrae of the neck to the fourth dorsal, the other a web section suspended on the cord and attached to all vertebrae between the second of the neck and the fourth dorsal.

sway-back. A concave curve of any part or all of the back line.

tarsal bones. A group of small bones forming the hock joint, the major one being the os calcis; tarsus or ankle.

tendon. A tough cord or band of inelastic tissue that connects the fleshy part of the muscle to the framework of the dog; sinew.

terrier front. Any front assembly with a normal shoulder blade and a short humerus or upper arm that permits the elbow to move freely above the brisket line.

thigh. The section of the back leg extending from the pelvis to the stifle joint and containing the femur. On dogs this is sometimes called the first thigh, and the section between the stifle and hock is called the second thigh instead of the gaskin, which the dictionary defines as the name for that section of the leg in quadrupeds.

thigh muscles. The forward action is produced mainly by the gluteus medius extending from the pelvis to the lower end of the femur, the profundus extending from the spine to the femur and the superficillis coming from the crown of the croup to the femur.

The backward action is due mainly to the biceps femoris arising on the croup, attached to the back of the pelvis and extending to the crown of the tibia and the semitendinosus which arises behind the femoris on the croup attaches to the pelvis tip and thence to the tibia.

thorax. The part of the body between the neck and the abdomen which is encased in the ribs; thoracic cavity contains the heart and lungs.

tibia. The front and larger of two bones in the gaskin or second thigh; the weight carrier and through it force is transmitted.

timing. The number of specific supports of the dog's body in one complete sequence of any gait; the gait taking its time rating from this number.

trapezius. A muscle, described in shoulder muscles.

triceps. Triangular muscles extending from the top half of the shoulder blade to the elbow with tendons continuing down the leg; it straightens the elbow and bends the shoulder joint, lifting the upper arm.

trot. A two-time movement made up of diagonal supports only; right front and left rear or left front and right rear.

tulip ear. An ear carried erect but having a tendency to curve forward along its sides.

vertebrae. Any of the single bones or segments composing the spinal column. From head to tail, they run: 7 cervical of neck, 8 dorsal of withers, 5 dorsal of back, 7 lumbar of loin, 3 fused sacral of croup and 5 to 22 cocygeal of tail.

walk. A four-time movement in which each of the four supports usually receive aid from one of the other supports.

well. This adjective is the beginning or part of numerous descriptive phrases applied to dogs, such as *well laid back shoulder,* and *well ribbed up.* The phrases are described elsewhere in their shorter form and this adjective, when it appears, is an emphasis on the feature.

wheel back. Any excessive convex curve of the back line.

withers. The first eight dorsal vertebrae to which the muscles of the shoulder blade are attached. The vertical spires of these vertebrae are longer than those of the back dorsals and by attachment they are a part of the shoulder assembly. Sometimes used to designate the peak of this section of vertebrae.

Index